Cracking
the
Code

10 Possible Reasons You Didn't Get the Job

B o b b y   M c N e i l   J r .

Cracking the Code: 10 Possible Reasons You Didn't Get the Job

Copyright © 2025 by Bobby McNeil Jr.

SHE PUBLISHING LLC and Bobby McNeil, Jr.

S.H.E. PUBLISHING, LLC

For information contact:
Email: info@shepublishingllc.com
Website: www.shepublishingllc.com

MUNSTER, INDIANA | INDIANAPOLIS, INDIANA

Book Cover and Title Page design by *Nabin Karna*

Cover Photo by *Morgan Crutchfield Photography*

Library of Congress Control Number: 2025944605

ISBN:
978-1-964061-34-4 (paperback)
978-1-964061-33-7 (hardback)

First Edition: September 2025

10 9 8 7 6 5 4 3 2 1

Disclaimer

Cracking the Code:
10 Possible Reasons You Didn't Get the Job

"The Career Book for The Culture"

*Please be advised that the views and perspectives expressed in this book **are strictly my own**. These views **do not** reflect the opinions or positions of any of my current or past employers, including organizations I was affiliated with before, during, or after the development and release of this book.*

- Bobby McNeil Jr.

Contents

Cracking
the
Code

10 Possible Reasons You Didn't Get the Job

Bobby McNeil Jr.

Introduction

The Career Book for The Culture

This isn't your typical career advice book…and honestly, it was never meant to be.

Cracking the Code: 10 Possible Reasons You Didn't Get the Job is part blueprint, part wake up call and real talk. It's for the job seekers navigating rejections, second-guessing their worth and wondering what more they could have done to finally get a yes. It's for the achievers who've done the work, but still feel like something's missing. It's for anyone tired of generic career advice that doesn't speak to the realities of today's job market.

I wrote this book for the overlooked; the qualified candidates who never get the callback; the professionals questioning if they're still relevant; the ones making career pivots, trying to figure out their next move, and just need a game plan that makes sense. Whether you're fresh out of school, making a big shift or bouncing back after a layoff, I see you. I've been you. And I want to help you.

This book leans heavily into *real stories from real people*, including true stories and scenarios that I've lived myself. These moments *actually happened.* The people are real, the situations are real and the lessons are real.

Over the course of my 16-year career, I've been on all sides of the hiring table: the candidate, the recruiter, the hiring manager and the talent strategist. I've helped people get hired in tech, engineering, finance, science, marketing, you name it. I've led national recruiting teams, coached & mentored recruiters, partnered with global brands and received numerous awards and accolades for my work in talent acquisition. I've sat in the rooms where decisions were made, and I've coached candidates through some of the most pivotal interviews of their lives; and yes, I've been through layoffs too. I've felt the pressure. I've felt the doubt and I've done the work to rebuild.

Some of the insights in this book are things I've spoken about at industry conferences across the country and on some of the most popular career and business podcasts online. Others? I've never spoken about them publicly, until now. These are gems, truths and reflections I've kept close until I knew the right time and format to share them. That time is now.

This book will not only help you understand the hiring process; it will help you understand the role you play in it. It will dispel false narratives, break down outdated assumptions and give you not just the *how* but also the *why*. Because the *why* is what most career books skip over, but it's what truly helps you grow and move with clarity.

Cracking the Code balances ***intellectual intrigue with cultural relevance.*** It's designed to make you think critically, reflect internally and most of all, see yourself in the stories and insights shared. It combines my **professional expertise** with my **creative and cultural lens**, using examples and metaphors that are relatable and rooted in real life, not vague buzzwords or corporate jargon that talks over your head.

This isn't a book filled with empty catchphrases and cookie-cutter templates. It's grounded, specific, human, and honest.

That's why it's nicknamed *The Career Book for The Culture.*

If you've ever felt stuck, unsure or simply ready to level up, welcome. You're not alone. It's the book I wish someone gave me years ago when I was trying to figure it all out.

— **Bobby McNeil Jr.**

Chapter 1

The Cold Front
When the Market Goes Silent

Reason #1: Cold Job Market

Hiring freezes and layoffs! Two things nobody wants to see pop up on their screen. It doesn't matter if it's from CNN, a Slack message from leadership or the subject line of a company-wide memo; those words hit hard. Even the most confident, most resilient among us pause when they hear them. For those who've already been through a layoff, those words don't just stop us dead in our tracks, those words echo loudly. Like a ghost from the past showing up again unannounced. Those old emotions creep right back up to the surface. That fear. The sting. That feeling of being caught off guard and losing it all.

Let's rewind to 2023, the year the job market caught frostbite. A record-breaking wave of layoffs swept through the country like a winter storm no one was fully ready for. Memos. Zoom calls. All hands meetings scheduled out of nowhere. One by one, inboxes filled up with calendar invites for "important updates". Some of us knew what that meant before we even clicked. It was like seeing the storm warning scroll across the bottom of your TV screen. You didn't need a weatherman to know the chill was setting in; the storm was here. The real fear was what could possibly come next; and like any storm, people reacted. Just like people rush to grab milk and bread before a snowstorm hits, many professionals scrambled to prep. Some updated their resumes. Some downloaded every job search tool they could find. Others poured a drink trying to numb the anxiety, hoping to ride it out. Either way, the signal was clear. The job market was entering deep freeze. Then came the blackout.

One moment, you're logged in, calendar full, emails flowing, and the next, everything's dark. Access denied. Email shut off. Slack silenced. Accounts closed. That dreaded message *"Your position has been impacted"* hits your inbox and spreads across your screen like a sheet of ice on a windshield; cold, heavy and impossible to ignore. The layoff email. The one that shuts down your professional power grid and leaves you sitting alone in silence and with a ton of questions. Many of us lived this very moment. Hundreds of thousands in the U.S. were laid off in 2023, many from the tech industry. Behind every number was a name. A story. A career suddenly got put on ice.

It wasn't just those already employed who felt it. There were already thousands of people deep in the job search before the layoffs hit. People networking, applying, interviewing. Suddenly, they were joined by a massive wave of talented professionals who were now also looking for work. The floodgates opened, and the competition tripled overnight. Now you're not just in a job search; you're navigating a frozen landscape, where opportunity feels scarce, the competition is fierce, and the odds feel stacked.

What happened was a shift. From a talent's market to an employer's market. Think of it like the housing market. When there are more homes than buyers, it's a buyer's market, meaning they have the power and get to be picky, choosing from dozens of options, and negotiate from a position of strength. However, when homes are scarce and buyers are lined up, it's a seller's market, meaning they set the terms, raise the price and hold the leverage. In a talent's market, job seekers move with more confidence. In an employer's market, companies move with more discernment.

So now that the storm has hit, the question becomes, 'How do you navigate it?' Before we get into survival strategies, let's check the forecast.

Forecast Check: Know What Market You're In

In a talent's market, job seekers hold the leverage. There are more openings than qualified candidates willing to fill them, and that shortage gives talent the advantage. Think of it like a stretch of warm weather. Doors of opportunities fly open, hot offers come in fast and companies go above and beyond to impress. Bigger sign-on bonuses than usual, fully remote roles at their choosing, personalized relocation packages and other perks. Candidates had leverage, some even juggling multiple offers at once. Recruiters were frantically chasing passive talent, sliding into DMs and inboxes for hours, hoping to catch the right person at the right time, but when the storm rolled in, everything shifted.

An employer's market is a different kind of forecast for job seekers. It's colder. Suddenly, there are more job seekers than there are actual jobs, and just like that, the power swings back to employers. The market turns cold fast, leaving hundreds of thousands of professionals out in the cold with resumes in hand, scrambling for shelter in the form of their next opportunity.

As a recruiter, I witnessed his firsthand. A single job post I would publish at noon could bring in 750 applications by 3PM, and I'm not even kidding. That's the mark of an employer's market. In times like these, active job seekers flood the pipeline. These are talented folks applying day and night, doing all the right things, hoping to stand out in a crowd that's growing by the minute.

The difference between these two climates is everything. Because the way you move in a heat wave is not the way you move in a blizzard. Recognizing the job market conditions around you helps you move with strategy, not just survival. Knowing when to pivot your approach is important in how you stay ready, no matter what the forecast says.

Before you start blaming yourself for the cold front, let's be real. The freezes in the job market didn't start because of you. So don't carry that weight. Just like you can't control the weather, you can't control market conditions either. What you can do is understand the storm and what causes these shifts, the freezes, the layoffs and why they're not a reflection of your worth.

The Real Behind the Chill

There are so many reasons why the job market can turn cold. Over the last 16 years, I've seen just about seen it all. I've seen hiring heatwaves where everybody was getting calls left and right, and I've seen deep freezes where everything came to a sudden stop. But some slowdowns just hit different. These are the ones that don't care if you're fresh out of school and eager to start, or an experienced professional finally close to that big step up. When the cold front comes in, it hits almost everyone in its path, no matter your level or background.

Whenever a slowdown hits, people reach out to me confused, hurt, and looking for answers. One person told me they had just wrapped up the best performance review of their career, got promoted and everything but just weeks later, they were laid off. For the most part, this person felt safe. Everything was looking up. Then out of nowhere, they too ended up out in the cold. Another job seeker shared how they went through the entire interview process for a role they were excited about, only to be told the company froze the position altogether.

There were moments I didn't have the words; and for someone people looked to for answers, that was hard. I was left speechless. I sat in the silence like everyone else, staring at the uncertainty, thinking to myself like, *maybe I should fall back for a minute, stay low and get some things together too like everyone else.* However, as someone who's been in the game for a while, I knew I had to understand it deeper. So, I tapped in with my network. Recruiters, executives and leaders; contacts that I trusted, that could help me piece it all together.

Sometimes, the job market just hits pause and when it does, it catches people off guard. One minute, companies are posting new roles by the dozen. The next? Everything slows down. Interviews stall. Roles that once felt like a perfect match suddenly vanish into thin air. But what really causes that kind of freeze?

There's no single reason. It's a mix of business moves and market anxiety happening behind the scenes. Sometimes it's rising costs or tightening budgets. Other times, it's uncertainty in the economy that causes companies to pull back and play it safe. Leadership might shift, projections might miss the mark, or business leaders might decide it's time to "wait and see." It's like a cold front blowing through the market. It's unpredictable, sharp, and chilling everything in its path.

That cold front doesn't just show up out of nowhere. It's often brought on by inflation, interest rate hikes, declining profits, or fears of a recession. And when the forecast looks cloudy, companies zip up the hiring jacket and put a hold on things, and board up everything in sight until the weather clears.

And here's what I need you to hear. It's not always about *you.* It's not because your resume missed the mark or your interview wasn't strong. A hiring freeze means the company is pausing to recalibrate. It's not personal.

Still, I get it. That doesn't make it feel any easier when you're in the middle of it. And it does feel personal. When you've prepped, showed up, crushed the interview, and then suddenly... nothing. You start refreshing your inbox. Replaying conversations in your head. Second-guessing what you said or didn't say. But more often than not, the silence has nothing to do with your qualifications; it's timing. It's budgets. It's market conditions, It's business decisions.

That kind of silence can mess with your head. But don't let it. A frozen job market isn't a reflection of your value. It's a reflection of a market trying to find its footing. You're still talented. You're still capable. You're still needed.

So, what do you do when the job market goes cold?

You bundle up and move wisely. You don't panic. You adjust your strategy, protect your mindset, and keep your confidence warm. Because while the forecast might be uncertain, your value isn't.

The goal isn't just to survive a hiring freeze; it's to navigate it. Cold fronts don't last forever, but how you move during them can set the tone for what happens when the ice melts. Here's how to stay sharp, stay seen, and stay ready while the market is on pause.

How To Crack the Code to a Cold Job Market

With all honesty, this is probably one of the more difficult codes to crack. Not because it's not possible, but because it is going to require a lot of patience, and most importantly acceptance of things that are beyond your control. This has more to do with what is going on around you. A cold job market brings hard times for many. There are ways to be more resilient. I've personally weathered a few icy markets in my day and even though each one was different, all of them required a tremendous amount of faith, grit, perseverance and belief in myself. The sobering reality is that there will be other seasons where you will have to hunker down and weather the blizzard. Because the storm doesn't ask permission; it just shows up. Below are some practical things you can do in case another icy job market comes your way.

Stay in Your Lane, Just Make It Wider

When the job market gets tight, it's not the time to box yourself in. If you've been laid off from a tech company just as an example, or if that promising tech role you were interviewing for suddenly froze mid-process, take a deep breath, zoom out and look at things more broadly. One thing I noticed in my consultations during that time was how many folks were laser-focused on landing a tech job in the tech industry. That's understandable, especially if that's where you built your experience. However, I want to challenge you to think bigger.

Tech isn't just a tech industry thing. It's an every industry thing now. Finance, healthcare, education, manufacturing, government. They all need tech talent. They've got stability, opportunity and a real need for people who know how to build, optimize and solve problems. Don't sleep on the smaller or privately held companies either. They also need smart, capable people just like you, and your skills might stand out even more in those environments.

You don't always have to pivot your role. Sometimes, the pivot is in the industry. So no, you don't have to abandon your lane, but in a frozen market, find ways to widen it.

The Sleeper Picks: Resilient Industries That Hold It Down

Tech that might get all the shine, but it's not bulletproof. I say that as someone who genuinely loves the tech industry. Out of all the industries I've touched, and trust me, it's been a few, tech is where I really made my mark and leveled up. The truth is, no industry is immune to hiring freezes or market declines, but some industries have a different kind of resiliency. They may not be flashy, trendy or go viral on LinkedIn, but they show up strong when the economy takes a plunge. They aren't always in the spotlight, but always in the fight.

If tech isn't your thing, no worries. There are plenty of non-technical roles across these sectors that align with your talents and can offer real career growth. It's not about abandoning your lane. It's about expanding your horizons.

When the job market turns cold, these industries keep the lights on. They offer a level of stability and job security that can be a lifeline, especially when everything else feels uncertain. Over the years, I've watched these industries stay steady while others shook. So, what I'm about to share isn't from a trending thread. It's from experience.

Utilities – Good in Any Storm: Think about it. When a real winter storm hits, what do we depend on most? Water, heat, electricity, trash pick-up. This industry keeps us warm, clean and functioning.

The utilities industry is the unsung hero of a snow day. In the same way, during an economic downturn, the utilities industry becomes a safe place. When everything else slows down or freezes up, this industry keeps moving. Why? Because everybody, from families to big business, still needs power, running water and waste management, no matter what the economy looks like. So, when the job market gets icy, don't sleep on the utilities industry. It's steady and essential. Sure, this industry isn't flashy, but it's built to weather the storm, and they'll always need people to help keep the lights on.

Healthcare – The Industry That Never Sleeps: If there's one industry I'd say is rock solid, it's healthcare. Hands down. No matter what the economy is doing, booming, crashing, or somewhere in between. That means healthcare keeps moving. From doctors and nurses to analysts, IT specialists, HR and administrative specialist, this industry runs on a wide variety of skill sets. I've seen firsthand how healthcare continues to hire when other sectors start freezing up. When the job market gets cold and uncertain, healthcare has often been the steady hand. This industry keeps people working and securing a paycheck while other industries are trying to figure it out.

Education – The Classroom Never Closes: When the job market turns cold, people turn to learning. People will use downtime to level up. Whether it's going back to school, getting that certification, or enrolling in a bootcamp, education becomes both the fallback plan and the bounce back plan. That's why the education sector from traditional universities to modernized e-learning platforms tends to stay steady even when other industries freeze up.

E-learning companies have built powerful digital campuses that are always open. They've become the go-to for folks looking to upskill, reskill, pivot or just sharpen up while they wait for the market to thaw. Because they're easily accessible, their demand only grows when hiring slows down. Parents still keep their kids in school, and adults turn into students again, enrolling and logging into classes from their phones, laptops and tablets during lunch breaks or during job search breaks. So, if you're looking for a lane that stays moving in any season, the education space might just be the warmest corner in a cold market.

Government – For the People, With the Perks: When the market goes cold, government jobs tend to stay warm. Whether it's local, state or federal, public-sector roles have long been known for their stability, solid benefits, and long-term perks like pensions and generous PTO. Regarding federal positions, the salaries can be surprisingly competitive. Sure, the government has had a few shutdowns over its hundreds of years of existence, but most of them barely last more than a handful of days before operations are back in motion. In the middle of a hiring freeze or job market downturn, working for "the people" often means having a little more peace of mind. The private sector may pause, but essential government work keeps moving.

Contracts & Side Hustles: Keep Food on the Table

One of the smartest plays you can make in a cold market is being open to contract work. After layoffs or hiring freezes, a lot of companies get really cautious about bringing on full-time staff. But projects still need to get done, deadlines still need to be met and that's where contractors come in. Short-term contracts, project-based roles or temp-to-perm setups give companies flexibility and provide a foot in the door for you. Contracting keeps your skills sharp, helps you stay current in a changing market and can even lead to something more permanent down the road.

Let's not forget your side hustle. In moments like this, the thing you've been doing after hours, whether it's design, consulting, selling products or creating content, might be the very thing that sustains you. You might just find that your side hustle isn't just a passion project. It's a business waiting to bloom.

After The Storm

All this talk about winter storms and cold markets has me thinking about some of my childhood summers down in Holly Springs, North Carolina in my late grandmother's little house with the gravel driveway. It was nothing fancy, but it was full of love. Back then, I was June Bob. That was my nickname, and that's what she called me. Long before I was a college basketball champion, a top recruiter, or featured on CNBC. Before the titles, the six figure salaries, the top 50 list, the board seats, or the stage lights. I was her skinny, quiet little grandson. The one she always said would do great things.

Back then in Holly Springs, you didn't have a weather app to know whether a storm was coming. You could smell it in the air; that humid smell that let you know rain was on the way. My grandma would call us inside that little house, sit us down, tell us to be quiet and turn off all the lights until the storm passed. If you grew up Black in the rural south, then you already know. That wasn't just about the storm outside. That was about safety and reverence. That stillness that taught us how to wait things out.

Once the skies cleared, we were back outside. Laughing like the storm never happened. Just being kids again under the Carolina sun. I can still hear the creak of that old screen door slamming behind me as we'd run in and out of the house. Inside, the smell of chicken and dumplings, family photos on the wall and as always in that little house of hers, old school gospel playing in the background. One song that she always played sticks with me to this day. *"Trouble Don't Last Always"* by the late Reverend Timothy Wright. That song wasn't just music. It was a reminder. A promise. A declaration that no matter what life threw your way, no storm was ever meant to last forever.

I didn't pay it any mind as a kid, but the message in that song hits different now. Because even with all my success, I know what it feels like to be in the middle of a cold season. I know what it feels like to be talented and driven; to have done everything right and still get hit with the layoff, or get ghosted after five rounds of interviews, or feeling like the market just froze up right when you were finally finding your rhythm.

Cold job markets don't always last. Hiring freezes don't always last. You still have power. You still have purpose, and you still have your mission. The storm can shake your confidence for a minute, but it can't take your hustle. So, keep going. Keep showing up. Keep believing. Even if things feel cold right now. Trust me, your season will come. When it does, everything you've been through will make sense. Because trouble don't last always… and neither do storms.

Chapter 2

Back to the Basics
Wants vs. Needs

Reason #2: Didn't Meet the Basic Requirements

I've grown to really appreciate those early days in my career before the titles, the speaking gigs or strategy sessions in the boardrooms. I was just trying to get in the door and prove I belonged. My recruiting journey officially started in 2009, the same year Kanye jumped on the VMA stage, when Obama took the oath for his first term and J. Cole, North Carolina's very own dropped *The Warm Up*, which became the soundtrack to my morning commutes. We also lost the King of Pop that year. The world felt like it was shifting, but for me, something was beginning.

I wasn't a recruiter just yet. I was a Recruiting Assistant at a staffing firm, doing all the behind-the-scenes work. Updating job postings, filing interview notes, learning how to source and making more coffee runs than I'd like to admit. I wasn't interviewing candidates or making job offers. I was laying the foundation, learning the basics, handling the not so glamorous but essential parts of the game that would shape everything I'd go on to do. It got frustrating at times. I knew I had potential. I felt like young Simba, letting out little roars here and there, just waiting on my moment to be King; but looking back, that season was necessary. It taught me patience, work ethic and how to build from the ground up.

There were no AI tools, no browser extensions and no advanced filters with chat boxes to find top talent. Boolean search strings were built by hand. ATS systems were basic. If you wanted to be great at this, you had to get it out the weeds; and I did. One of the biggest turning points during that time? Job descriptions. At first, I was just posting them, but eventually, I was helping to write them from scratch. That small task opened doors, giving me a seat at the table with hiring managers, senior recruiters and sometimes even executives. I didn't take that lightly. I knew the more I learned, the more valuable I'd become. So, I leaned in, asked smart questions and came to meetings ready with most of the answers already in my back pocket.

Fast forward to today, and honestly, not much has changed in the conversations I'm having. Whether I was the rookie Recruiting Assistant grinding it out in my agency days or now sitting at the table as a Recruiting Leader, one topic that always finds its way into the mix is the "job requirements" section of the job description. Back then, I was just trying to understand what to post. Now, I'm helping teams decide what really needs to be there in the first place.

When I meet with hiring managers, we dive deep, breaking down what the actual bar is- for candidates to be seriously considered. When I'm out in the community or just chopping it up with friends in the group chat, the energy is different. For job seekers, those same requirements often feel like a wall. A long list that looks like you need five degrees, ten certifications and a purple squirrel on your resume just to get a callback.

At the heart of it, it all comes down to the same thing; wants vs. needs. Hiring managers are thinking in terms of "must-haves" and "nice-to-haves." Job seekers are trying to figure out what actually matters and if they're even in the ballpark. I've seen job descriptions so long they look like those chaotic grocery lists you scribble on Thanksgiving Eve with every random item thrown in there, but I've also seen beautifully written ones that help candidates make sense of where they stand.

From every angle. The young and hungry assistant triple-checking each bullet point before posting, the recruiter having tough conversations with candidates who don't quite meet the bar, the leader brought in to reshape the strategy and even the hiring manager trying to build a team of recruiters, I've lived all sides of the spectrum.

The truth is, not checking every single box doesn't mean you're not qualified. What matters more is knowing which boxes actually move the needle. All roads, whether you're searching for a job or trying to level up, eventually bring you back to the basics. You either figure out what's been blocking your progress, or you finally find the clarity that's been missing.

The Truth Behind the Checkboxes

Job requirements usually serve two main purposes. One for the recruiter, the other for the job seeker. For recruiters, they act like a quick screening tool. A checklist to help them make sure they're bringing solid candidates to the hiring manager. For job seekers, they're more like a benchmark. A snapshot of what it really takes to succeed in the role once you're hired. If you've been in the game long enough, you've probably learned to separate the list into two buckets: the essentials and the extras. Or as we like to call them, the "must-haves" and the "nice-to-haves."

On paper, they're labeled as "Basic Requirements" and "Preferred Qualifications." Basic requirements are exactly what they sound like, the bare minimum. These are the non-negotiables; core skills, experiences and credentials that are critical to doing the job well from day one. They're the engine under the hood. The things that keep the role moving. Then there's preferred qualifications. That's where the seasoning comes in. They aren't mandatory, but they add flavor. Think of them like bonus points. The things that elevate your candidacy and show you're bringing something extra to the table. They're not deal-breakers, but definitely give you a leg up if you have them.

Here's what most people don't realize. Job requirements aren't just randomly pulled out of thin air. They come from real conversations behind the scenes. I've been in those rooms. I've helped lead those talks. Whether I was partnering with hiring managers as a recruiting leader or talent mapping roles as a manager myself, I've seen just how much thought and dialogue goes into writing that one little section on a job post. Sometimes there's back and forth, debates even, on what's truly necessary versus what's just wishful thinking. In the end, it usually comes down to a few key drivers that shape what ends up on that final list. Here are some of them.

The Needs of the Business – Like I mentioned earlier, some skills, experiences and levels of knowledge aren't just helpful, they're non-negotiable. These are the things that don't just help a new hire succeed, they help the whole team stay afloat and keep business moving. When a department is missing a key skill set, it's not just a minor gap, it can create ripple effects that hit multiple areas of the organization, especially when the role is high-exposure or very cross-functional, getting the right person in place is critical. That's why hiring managers take these requirements seriously. It's not about creating a checklist just to make things harder. It's about making sure the business has what it needs to operate at its highest level.

Workload & Team Structure – Sometimes job requirements have less to do with the job itself and more to do with the bigger picture. I've sat in plenty of meetings where the hiring manager wasn't just focused on what the new person would do. They were also focused on who the team already had. They're trying to figure out what's missing, what strengths the team has too much of and where the gaps are. It's like putting together a starting five. You can't have five point guards on the floor. You need a squad with different skill sets that complement each other. Someone who can shoot, someone who can defend, someone who can lead. The same goes for building a team at work. They're trying to round out the team so the whole unit performs better. When you see a job description, just know that some of what you're reading is based on what the team needs right now to keep winning.

Hiring History & Lessons Learned – Another thing that shapes job requirements is good old hindsight. Sometimes a role has already been filled before, and maybe more than once. How that person showed up in the role leaves a mark. Maybe they struggled and left gaps that hurt the team. Either way, those experiences leave behind a trail of lessons, which almost always show up in the next job description. I've sat in on plenty of these conversations where the hiring manager says, "Last time, we missed the mark on XYZ," It's not about throwing requirements on paper just to keep people out. It's about refining what's needed based on what the team's already been through. Whether it's tweaking a skill, adding a certification, or rewording something to be more clear, it's all rooted in learning from the past to make a stronger hire for the future.

Understanding how job requirements are crafted can be a game changer in your job search. Over the years, from my early days learning the ropes, to now leading recruitment strategies, I've had a front row seat to how job descriptions really come together. If there's one thing I've learned, it's this; not every "requirement" on that list is created equal, but you wouldn't know that unless you've been behind the scenes.

A lot of job seekers psych themselves out because they think they need to check every single box just to be considered. I used to be one of them. I remember those early job hunts. Eager, hopeful, ambitious, but if I didn't meet 100% of what was listed, I'd count myself out. I'd do a quick scan, spot two or three things I didn't have and close the tab. Just like that, opportunity missed. I was screening myself out before anyone else ever had a chance to. That's a quiet kind of rejection we don't talk about enough. A failure to launch that's rooted in doubt, not ability.

Once I got into recruiting and started seeing how descriptions really get built, and what hiring managers really care about, my whole mindset shifted. I stopped chasing perfection and started positioning my strengths around what actually moved the needle. That's when the doors started opening.

Here's the truth! You're not expected to be a perfect match. What matters is being able to spot the real must haves; the heavy hitters and showing how your skills align. That's how you move from hesitation to action. So, let's talk about what to focus on when you're sizing up your next opportunity.

Education Requirements – What the Paper Really Means

Let's talk about one of the most misunderstood job requirements out there. The education requirement. At a basic level, this box gets checked to make sure candidates have a certain level of foundational knowledge. It's less about having a fancy piece of paper and more about showing that you've mastered the concepts needed to operate in the space. Now, not every job is going to demand a college degree, especially not in today's market, but in most professional roles, there's at least an unspoken expectation that you've finished high school or earned your GED.

Where things get real is in more specialized roles in functions like tech, healthcare, finance and engineering. These lanes often require a bachelor's degree, certifications or even licenses; not because the company wants to make things hard, but because these fields come with standards that can't be skipped over. It's not just about what you know, it's about what you're trusted to do based on that knowledge. Sometimes, those credentials are what open doors and put you in the running in the first place.

Years of Experience – Time Served & Value Added

At the end of the day, the experience requirement is about receipts. It's how hiring managers confirm that you've been in the field, done the work and delivered real results. They want to see that you've actually been in the trenches, not just watching from the sidelines. When a job description says, "X years of experience," it's not just a number, it's a signal. It tells them you've been through enough business cycles to understand the rhythm of the role. That you've made some plays, taken some losses, bounced back and learned along the way.

A key principle I've learned after years on both sides of the table; it's about depth over duration. Just because someone's been locked in for seven years, doesn't mean they've grown for seven years. Hiring managers aren't just looking for bodies who've sat in a seat for a certain period. They want people who made an impact while they were there. If you've built real skills, made measurable impact and can speak to your wins, then you've got something to say.

The Skills Required – These Ain't Optional

Out of all the basic qualifications, this is the one that gets put under the biggest microscope. These are the tools in your bag. The ones you need to actually do the work. Without them, you're just not going to be able to function in the role. Period. There's no other way to put it. These aren't the "would be nice" type of skills. Not in this section. These are the "you gotta have it" to even stand a chance and stay afloat.

Most of the time, these show up as technical. They will reveal themselves as coding languages, data analysis tools, design software, lab techniques. Whatever's tied directly to the work; if it's a digital or STEM-based role, expect these to be front and center. And to keep it real; you will get tested. Some interviews will test your skills right on the spot. In a "what would you do" kind of way, or in a "go ahead and show us right now" kind of way.

Specialization Requirement – In The Deep End

Every now and then, a role calls for more than just solid skills and experience. It calls for your area of expertise. That's where the specialization requirement comes in. It's not just about doing the work; it's about knowing the work on a deeper level, being the go-to person in a very specific lane. This is when a company needs someone with a high level of subject matter expertise, someone who can bring insight, provide strategic guidance and operate as the resident expert. Think about it like this: they're not just hiring a Human Resources Manager. They need someone who's handled Industrial Labor Unions before and understands the nuance. In tech, they don't just want any software engineer. They need a backend systems specialist who can architect the foundation of an entire platform. This kind of requirement adds weight to the role.

Now, those key requirements I just walked you through, the education, experience, skills and specialization requirements, I call those The Fab 4, because in every job description I've reviewed, every role I've helped fill and every hiring decision I've been part of, those four show up and show out the most. They're the foundation, the main ingredients. More often than not, they're listed right at the top for a reason. Employers want you to see them first and weigh yourself against them early.

I've been on both sides of this. As the eager job seeker overthinking every bullet point, and as the seasoned recruiter scanning resumes looking for those big four. If you've got The Fab 4, don't hesitate. Click apply. Let the rest play out in the process.

Now, the rest of that requirements list, the "strong communication," "collaborative mindset," "strategic thinker" kind of stuff? Those are real and they are important, but they come in later in the interview. That's your moment to show and tell. So don't count yourself out too early. If you've got The Fab 4, you've got a reason to shoot your shot.

How to Crack the Code to Meeting the Basic Requirements

I know what it's like to get that dreaded rejection email. It stings. I've been there more than once in my career, but I've also sat on the other side of the table, making hiring decisions, weighing team dynamics and trying to find the right match. So, I get both sides. The frustration of the job seeker, and the pressure that comes with trying to get the right hire.

When you're in the thick of the job search, I absolutely believe in casting your net wide. Explore your options. See what's out there, but don't just apply blindly to every listing you come across. That's like pulling up to a sneaker drop without checking the release details. No idea about the colorways, specs or what sizes are available- just aimlessly hoping something fits. Anybody in that culture knows, that's not how you move if you're serious about the game.

Applying for jobs works the same way. You've got to move with intention. Be strategic. Show that you understand the space. Recruiters and hiring managers can spot someone who's just throwing their resume at anything. In tight knit industries, that can hurt your reputation over time. You don't want to be known as the candidate who applies to every role but doesn't read the fine print.

Serious sneakerheads don't chase every pair. They do their research. They know their sizes, the history behind the design and whether the fit actually works for their collection. That's how you've got to treat your job search. Know your fit. Know your strengths. Read over the details and go after roles that make sense and are a good fit.

Now let's shift gears and talk about something that can really change the game in your job search: reading between the lines. Just like a sneakerhead knows there's more to a release than what's on the box, the materials, the story behind the design, the resale buzz. A job description has layers too. It's more than just a list of tasks and qualifications. The way it's written can tell you a lot about what the company really needs. The order of the bullets, the tone, the words they emphasize (or leave out). They're all small clues. Once you learn how to pick up on those signals and decode the job description, you start making smarter, making more intentional moves. That's how you stop chasing just anything and start aiming for the right fit. So, let's break this down. Let me show you how to read a job post like someone who's done this before and help you move closer to the bullseye.

Don't Judge the Job by Its Title

The title might catch your eye first, but don't let it be the only thing that guides your decision. Just because a job has "Manager," "Director," or "Lead" in the name doesn't always mean you'll be managing people. Sometimes those titles are more about managing processes, overseeing projects or owning a function; not leading a team of direct reports. That leadership may be more about influence than authority.

If people management is part of the job, trust me, it'll show up in the experience section. If it says something like "must have experience managing a team," and you've done that? Go ahead and shoot your shot. However, if you haven't, ask yourself; *would I feel confident answering questions about this in an interview? Would I be stretching the truth to say I'm ready?*

Now, on the flip side, and this is where a lot of talented people miss out. If a title sounds big, like a "Manager" role for example, but there's no mention of directly managing people in the requirements, don't let that scare you off. So many qualified candidates pass up amazing opportunities because they assume they aren't "manager" enough, when really, they have what it takes to lead through influence.

So, from now on, don't get stuck on the title. Dig deeper and keep decoding, because sometimes, what sounds like a stretch is actually the perfect next step.

There's Levels to This

In the job search, titles tell one story, but levels? That's where the real clues are hidden when you're trying to decode what those individual contributor roles are really all about. When you see words like Senior or Principal baked into the title, don't just gloss over those. That's the company giving you a heads up on the caliber they're aiming for. A Principal title? That's not just a flex. It's signaling for some who brings serious expertise. These are the subject matter experts, those who leadership leans on for guidance, strategy and that next level insight. They're not always managers, but always respected voices in the room.

Now, when you see Senior, think heavy hitter. Someone who's been around the block, knows how to move without any handholding, and can take on big responsibilities with confidence. Senior level professionals are expected to bring experience, work independently and solve problems without needing a play by play from management. These roles aren't for beginners. They're for those who can walk in on day one and contribute like they've been there for months.

The Quick Filters

When it comes to decoding the Fab 4, we talked about earlier; education, experience, skills and specialization, just know these aren't just words tossed into the posting to take up space. These are the true filters. Most of the time, they show up as knockout questions in the ATS. You've probably seen them: *Do you have a Bachelor's degree in ___? Do you have X years of experience doing ___? Have you worked with ___ system before?* These questions are built to quickly filter candidates. If you answer "yes," you move forward. If it's a "no," it might flag your application or slow things down.

Now with AI being added to the mix, more systems are using ranking tools to score and sort candidates, but let me be real clear. AI might help streamline things, but it doesn't replace human judgment. Recruiters should still review what comes through; and trust me, if you hit the Fab 4, you're more likely to make it into that "take a closer look" list. Is it a guaranteed callback? No, but it definitely gives your application the kind of weight that makes someone pause and pay attention. It's all about improving your odds, and in a competitive job market, every edge counts.

Let's not sleep on the Preferred Requirements. No, they're not part of the Fab 4, and they won't automatically knock you out the running if you don't have them. But don't brush them off when you see them on the job description either. Think of them as the company's way of saying, *"If we bring you on, here's where we hope you'll grow."* These aren't just wish list items; they're subtle clues about the direction of the role and how the team or business is evolving. If you're serious about leveling up, this section can and should be viewed as a roadmap for your professional development in the role. So even if you don't check every preferred box right now, take note. It might just show you where your next stretch goals should be if selected.

From here on out, you're not just tossing your resume into the wind and hoping for the best. You're moving different now. You've got insight, you've got strategy and most importantly, you've got clarity. Every job posting drops gems. Little signals about what the company wants versus what it really needs. Now that you know how to decode, you can move smarter, not harder. The closer you align with the essential Fab 4, the better your chances are of getting that call back. So, stay locked in. Keep your aim steady, but this time, with intention. The foundation is set. The basics are clear.

Chapter 3

The Swiss Army Knife
Transfer Your Skills, Shift the Game

Reason #3: Non-Transferable Business Skills

L et's talk about the Swiss Army Knife for a second. That little tool is a legend, not because it's flashy or high-tech, but because it's useful. Very useful. Inside that small frame, you'll find everything from blades and scissors to a nail file, screwdrivers, bottle opener, even a can opener, all packed into one small but powerful package. It's built to do more than one thing. It's versatile, efficient and always ready for whatever comes its way. That's what makes it iconic.

I never owned a Swiss Army Knife myself, but trust me, they were a staple in the hands of the men who raised me. My dad, Bobby Sr., and my uncles swore by them. Where I come from, small-town North Carolina, tools like that weren't just useful, they were essential. They'd pull those things out at family cookouts, backyard bonfires or Saturday morning projects. One minute it was slicing open a cardboard box, scaling fish for the Friday night fish fry, the next it was tightening a screw or trimming a carpet edge. It wasn't flashy, but it was reliable. In a world where you had to be ready for anything, that little knife felt like a symbol, a quiet flex of resourcefulness.

It wasn't just our family. The Swiss Army Knife had a presence in the culture too. If you grew up in the '80s or caught the reruns later on, then you remember *MacGyver*. The cool quick-thinking guy on TV who could escape a hostage situation using only a Swiss Army Knife. It became more than a tool. It became a metaphor. A way to describe someone who had a little bit of everything in their bag. Someone who could pivot, adapt and handle whatever was thrown their way. That's the kind of value we're talking about when we mention transferable skills. Just like the Swiss Army Knife, your range and versatility as a professional can make you useful in almost any room you walk into. In a changing job market? That kind of adaptability is everything. If there's one thing I've learned, it's that hard skills will get you in the door, but it's your transferable business skills that'll help you move laterally, upwardly or into rooms you didn't even know you. Sometimes, that truth doesn't hit from a TED Talk or a team meeting. Sometimes it hits over steak and low lights in the middle of the city.

One Saturday night in Washington D.C.; it was one of those warm weather weekends in The District. There was something different in the air. I was in town speaking on an industry panel discussion, and had just wrapped a full day of work, networking and wandering through some of my favorite parts of Chocolate City. Out of nowhere, I got a text from an old friend. Brilliant, driven and gorgeous. If there was ever a "tech baddie", she was it. We'd always had a solid connection, even if life and busy schedules had us moving in different directions over the years.

There's always been a certain vibe between us. Nothing ever confirmed, but never fully denied either. That kind of energy. So, when I saw her name pop up on my phone, I won't lie, I smiled a bit. We made plans to meet at one of our favorite steakhouses. The kind of spot with white tablecloths, dim lighting and an upscale dress code that forces you to leave the Jordans back at the hotel. So, I went with the Chelsea boots and the classic, yet perfectly tailored black blazer.

I got there first, grabbed us a seat at the bar and waited. She texted to say traffic had her Uber tied up, but she'd be there soon. I texted her back to say no worries. It gave me a moment to sit in the energy of the restaurant. Then she walked in, and listen, she wasn't trying too hard, but somehow still lit up the room. We hugged like we'd done a hundred times before, but this one lingered just a second longer.

Over drinks and ribeyes, we reminisced about old times and how proud we were of each other's individual successes. The convo eventually got deep. She opened up about work. Told me how, even with her technical skills being on point and with results to show, she kept getting passed over for promotions and opportunities on other teams. She said, "I just don't get it, Bobby. I do the work. I know I'm good at what I do, but somehow, I'm still not moving up."

I listened, nodded and let her vent. Then I hit her with some real talk. Not just as her friend, but as someone who's lived through the same frustration. I told her that for the longest time, I thought being technically excellent was the only thing that mattered. I thought if I just delivered, people would notice, but promotions don't just go to the ones who get the job done. They go to the ones who understand the business, who can speak the language of leadership, who build bridges between teams, who can influence without needing a title.

She paused, took a sip of her expresso martini, then admitted something I already sensed. "I know I come off smart. Sometimes too smart, but I struggle when I have to explain things to non-technical people. It's like I hit a wall."

I leaned in closer to her and told her that the moment she figures out how to translate her intellect in ways that resonate beyond her bubble, doors would start to open. Because in this game, it's not just about what you know, it's how you connect.

I reminded her that her intellect wasn't in question, but growth, true growth sometimes lives in learning how to flex and use different tools. Skills even. That's what leaders do. They don't just execute, they elevate. Then I said to her, "Be like a Swiss Army Knife. All those sharp technical skills you got? Those are great, but it's the other tools like communication, influence, strategic thinking. Lean into those more."

We stayed posted at that bar longer than either of us expected. The food had been cleared, but the conversation kept flowing, no awkward pauses, no checking the time. Just good energy. Eventually, I glanced at my phone and realized how late it had gotten. I had an early flight back to Raleigh in the morning, and I still had to pack. I paid the bill and stepped out into the warm D.C. night. She looked up at me, smiled real soft, and said, "Thanks... I really needed this." I nodded and said, "Yeah... me too."

Some time had passed since that night in D.C. Life did what it always does. It kept moving. We both entered new seasons, new goals and even new relationships that came and went, but every now and then, we'd check in. A quick like on a post, a "Proud of you" in the comments, or a random text just to say what's up. She always kept an eye on my journey, and truth be told, I did the same with hers.

Then one day, months later, I saw it. She posted on LinkedIn that she'd been promoted. My mind instantly went back to that Saturday night at D.C., the conversation, the vibe, the way we locked in. I hit "like" on the post like everybody else, but for her, that wasn't enough. I had to send a text. *Congrats on the promotion. Proud of you.* Her reply came back quick: *I'll always appreciate you, Bobby! Thanks for helping me crack the code. #SwissArmyKnife LOL.*

I just stared at the message for a minute, smiling, because in that moment, I knew she got it. It's about learning how to flex those transferable skills. That's what makes you valuable in any setting, whether you're trying to level up, move sideways or pivot altogether.

The Swiss Army Skillset

Think of your transferable skills as that universal keycard that gets you past velvet ropes, backstage entrances and into rooms where your name might not be on the list yet. They're not just about technical know-how, though that plays its part. These are the business minded skills that follow you wherever you go, leveling you up across industries and roles, no matter your background. They're the secret sauce that makes people see you in a different light.

Pair these skills with your technical know-how, and suddenly, you're not just a specialist, you're a strategic force. You're no longer just in the conversation, you're leading it. Whether you're climbing the corporate ladder, pivoting to a new industry, or building your own lane as an entrepreneur, these business-savvy skills are like your Swiss Army Knife. Compact, reliable, sharp, and always ready to be pulled out when the moment calls for it.

So, before we unpack what the most valuable and transferable business skills actually are, take a second and understand this. These skills aren't just nice-to-haves. They're need-to-haves if you want to elevate. They're what take you from being a doer of task to being a driver of outcomes. The list I'm about to walk you through isn't just a checklist, It's a toolkit; and while it covers a lot, just know the game is constantly evolving, so sharpening these skills is never a one-time thing.

Project Management: Making Moves with a Plan

When most people hear "project management," they think Gantt charts and color-coded spreadsheets, but at its core, project management is really about bringing order to the chaos and doing it in a way that actually gets results. It's the ability to take something from idea to execution, keeping everything and everyone in sync from start to finish. That means setting clear milestones, tracking progress, managing timelines, and making sure the goal doesn't just look good on paper, but it gets done, and done right.

Data Analysis: Let the Numbers Talk

In today's workplace, the ability to break down data and make it make sense is one of the realist and most slept on skills when it comes to career mobility. Data analysis, sometimes referred to as analytical reasoning, isn't just a skill reserved for people with "analyst" in their job titles. It's about being able to take raw numbers, spot trends, pull insights and help drive smart, informed decisions for business leaders. That's not just good business, it's good strategy.

Effective Communication: Having A Good Talk Game

If there's one transferable skill that reigns supreme across every profession, it's effective communication. It doesn't matter what industry you're in, what your title says, or how long you've been doing the work. If you can't communicate clearly, concisely and with intention, it's going to hold you back. No questions asked.

Structured Problem-Solving: Let's Get to the Bottom of It

Structured problem-solving is all about pulling up with a game plan. It's not just reacting to things; it's knowing how to move with intention when things go left. It's about using a step-by-step approach to find the root cause of a problem, weigh the risks and figure out the clearest path forward. Employers eat this up, not because it's flashy, but because it works. Whether you're fresh out of college or a seasoned vet, whether you're on the creative side or in operations, this is one of those skills that earns respect everywhere.

Management: More Than Just Telling PeopleWhat to Do

When people hear the word "management," the first thought that comes to mind is usually about being the boss, overseeing a team, calling the shots and handing out tasks. Sure, that's part of it, but management is also way deeper than that. Strong management skills are about taking full ownership of the team, the process and the outcome. It's about having a clear vision, being able to delegate when necessary and knowing how to get results through others. It also means being willing to take accountability when things don't go according to plan. Whether the project was a hit or missed the mark, a true manager owns it all. Don't get it twisted. Management isn't just about people. In many cases, you might not be managing a team of people at all. You might be managing a budget, a process, a product line or even a massive data system.

Leadership: Influence Over Authority

Leadership hits different than management. It's not just about having your name at the top of the org chart or holding a big title. Some people might be seen as "natural born leaders," but for most of us, it's a skill that is learned and built over time, shaped through life experiences, through lessons or through repetitions. Leadership isn't always about power or control over people or resources. It's about impact. It's about your ability to move the needle, shift energy and get people to buy into a vision. It's being able to step up, even when it's not your job, and rally people behind a mission, a cause or a moment.

Strong transferable business skills can shift the entire trajectory of your career. They're what help you leap from the familiar into unknown territory without falling flat. Whether you're making a bold pivot, changing industries or just aiming for a higher level within your lane, these skills are what help tip the scale in your favor.

But here's the real key to all of this. Having these skills is only half the battle. The other half is being able to spot them within yourself, name them with confidence and speak on them in ways that connect. Whether it's in your resume, in an interview or while networking, you've got to know how to tell your story in a way that highlights what you bring to the table.

Now that we've walked through what these skills are, let's talk about how to recognize them in your own journey. You may have more of these skills than you realize.

How To Crack the Code to
Non-Transferable Business Skills

Whether you're early in your career looking to elevate or an experienced professional looking to pivot, transferable skills carry weight. They help you move the needle even when your resume may not check every box. I've seen this firsthand in my career, whether I was advocating for a promotion on behalf of someone on my team or sitting at the table with senior leaders discussing who's next up. The truth is, when it's time to talk promotions or leadership moves, we don't just talk about who does the job well, we talk about who gets the bigger picture, who brings strategy, who can communicate across teams, who influences and who makes people around them better.

You can be great at your job, but if you're not showing up as business savvy, you're playing small. The people who rise, the ones who get tapped for the next big opportunity, are the ones who bring more than just technical skill or tactical know-how. They bring vision, leadership and the ability to connect the dots. It's not just about being good at what you do anymore. It's about showing that you can help others win too. That's how you move from tactical mode to strategy mode. In this next section, we're going to walk through exactly how these skills might already be showing up in your career journey and how to spot, sharpen and put them to use.

Let's start with *Project Management*. Now here's the thing. You don't need "Project Manager" in your title to have this skill. If you've ever taken the lead on something at work like launching a new program, coordinating an event, improving a process, or even managing a vendor relationship, then you were running point. That's project management in real life. Whether you were mapping out steps, handling multiple tasks or rallying people across different departments, you were already doing the work.

Now, if you really want to sharpen this skill, certifications like the PMP or even foundational courses can give you a deeper understanding and help you speak the language in rooms where those distinctions matter, but don't underestimate your everyday wins. Project management is about showing you can keep things moving, even when things get messy. It's one of those transferable skills that proves you're not just a thinker. You keep things moving. The type who doesn't just talk about the play, you run it.

Next up is *Data Analysis*. I've learned firsthand, especially stepping into leadership roles, that making decisions on feelings alone simply won't cut it. You need receipts. The kind that come from data you've tracked, cleaned up and made plain for others to see. Whether it's deciding where to invest resources, how to improve team performance or figuring out why something just isn't working. Data helps you see the full picture. It turns your intuition into influence. Trust me, the higher up you go, the more people expect you to speak the language of numbers.

This isn't just about pivot tables and dashboards either. It's about showing that you can take what you've gathered whether its sales numbers, customer trends, hiring metrics, or project milestones and presenting it in a way that tells a story. A story that helps your team move, that helps executives decide and that earns you credibility in rooms you want to be in.

So, think back to when was the last time you pulled data to back up a recommendation? When did you gather results and use that to make your case stronger? Those moments matter. They're receipts for how you think, how you lead and how you move.

Being data-driven doesn't make you stiff. It makes you sharp. Because when you can back up your strategy with proof, you're not just talking, you're walking with credibility; and that's what leaders do.

Now *Effective Communication* is a real game changer. You'll see it in almost every job description, usually tucked somewhere between the technical skills and qualifications, but don't get it twisted. That bullet point isn't just there for decoration. It's there because communication is the bridge between great ideas and real impact. I've seen brilliant professionals get overlooked, simply because they couldn't articulate their value in a way that resonated. I've also seen people with average technical skills soar because they knew how to connect, influence and rally a room around what they were saying. In your career journey, effective communication shows up in more ways than just polished emails or big presentations. It's in the way you navigate a virtual one-on-one, how you handle a tense conversation with a client, the clarity in your project updates or even the patience you show when listening to someone explain a complex challenge. Maybe it's you leading the slide deck during a team strategy session, translating highly technical ideas in a room full of non-technical people or moderating an engaging discussion where every voice needs to be heard. That's communication and that's leadership. When you master this skill, you're not just speaking on information, you're building trust. Trust is the true currency in this professional game.

So, take note of how well you connect across teams. Can you curate your message for different audiences? Can you listen as well as you speak? The ability to communicate with clarity and purpose doesn't just make you more effective; it makes you more valuable.

Now let's talk about one of the skills that doesn't always get the spotlight, *Structured Problem-Solving*. Before I started recruiting for tech roles like software engineers, cybersecurity analysts or IT business partners, my career was spent recruiting a lot of non-technical talent. I was recruiting sales professionals, marketing creatives, scientists, mechanical engineers, you name it. I've don't it all. That wide lens taught me a lot. I kept hearing the same methods mentioned across industries: project managers in Pharma using DMAIC, engineers talking about root causes with Fishbone Diagrams and even operations leaders leaning into PDCA for improving processes. So, by the time I stepped into recruiting in the tech space, I already had a deep bench of tools I'd heard about or seen in action.

Let me break down a few of the most common structured problem-solving methods I've seen out there, because odds are, you've used one and didn't even know it had a name:

- **DMAIC** (Define, Measure, Analyze, Improve, Control): This one's a classic in the Lean Six Sigma playbook and is mainly used in manufacturing or process-heavy environments. Think of it like climbing the ranks in martial arts. Yellow Belt is basic, Green Belt is intermediate, and Black Belt is expert. Each belt represents your ability to attack problems and improve how things run.

- **PDCA** (Plan, Do, Check, Act): This one's been around since the 1950s thanks to Dr. Deming. It's simple but effective. Make a plan, try it, evaluate it, then adjust and repeat. You'll see it everywhere from continuous improvement projects to operations teams trying to tighten things up.

- **SWOT Analysis** (Strengths, Weaknesses, Opportunities, Threats): You've probably heard of this one in business class or during planning sessions. It's used to figure out if a new idea, project, or initiative is even worth pursuing. You look at what's working, what's missing, what's possible, and what might go wrong.

- **The 5 Whys**: Don't overthink this one. It's literally asking "why" five times. It's what curious little kids and wise professionals have in common. It helps get past surface-level answers to uncover what really caused a problem in the first place.

- **The Fishbone Diagram**: This one maps out all the possible causes of a problem in a way that looks like a fish skeleton. It's especially big in quality control, but I've seen teams use it to brainstorm across departments too.

- **The Decision Tree**: Think of a flowchart but make it strategic. It maps out your options and the outcomes that come with each one. Whether you're choosing a vendor or picking a weighing out a business move, this helps you see the big picture clearly.

Some of these might feel familiar, like something you've done in a past role or even in your personal life. Others may be brand new to you. If you've ever solved a tough problem by following steps, discussing smart tradeoffs and finding a real solution, then you've already got this skill. Structured problem-solving is one of the most valuable skills you can carry in your toolkit, and it transfers across roles, industries and functions. It shows you're not just guessing, but rather, you're thinking, strategizing and building your career like a real one. Keep sharpening it. The doors it can open might surprise you.

Let's move on to talk about probably the most misunderstood skill set. *Management*. Whether you're supervising headcount or overseeing resources, the responsibility and skillset still apply. That's why the management skill set travels so well across functions and is universal. If you can manage a process in one industry, you can often adapt and do the same in another. The truth is that management isn't always loud. It doesn't always look like someone standing at the front of the room giving orders. Sometimes it's the quiet work of making decisions under pressure, catching a mistake before it spreads or finding a way to stretch limited resources without sacrificing quality. That's management too. So, whether you're leading people, projects or platforms. The ability to manage effectively is a transferable skill that gets noticed and one that can help you cross industries, climb ladders and get your name called when it's time to level up.

Last but definitely not least, let's get into *Leadership,* because real leadership has never been about titles. You don't need a title to lead. Think back when maybe you were the one who stepped in when something was falling apart. Maybe you were the calm voice during the chaos or the motivator when your team felt stuck. That's leadership. In today's world, that kind of influence is valuable. Employers are looking for it. Teams respond to it and people remember it. The beauty of leadership is that it transfers across industries and roles, and it even shows up in how you carry yourself outside of work. Whether you're leading a strategy session or organizing the next family reunion, the skills are the same. Vision. Empathy. Initiative. That's all it takes. It's a timeless trait that opens doors, earns trust and separates you from the crowd.

As you've seen by now, transferable skills aren't just buzzwords or fillers in a job description or resume. They're your career's Swiss Army Knife; compact, reliable, useful and timeless. When sharpened, they're powerful enough to cut through any challenges along our career journey. They take you from being the doer who checks boxes to the decision maker who shapes strategy. From someone busy completing tasks to someone intentional about how their work drives the bigger picture forward. These skills help you go from simply showing up to standing out because you're no longer just reporting updates, you're recommending solutions. You're not just booked and busy, you're intentional, clear and impactful. The truth is, no matter where you are in your career; leveling up, or pivoting to something new, your ability to leverage these business minded skills will make people remember your name and your work. So, keep sharpening your Swiss Army Knife. Keep stacking those skills, because when the opportunity comes, you won't just be in the room you'll be ready to stand out in it.

Chapter 4

Press Play
Your Resume Is the Hype Reel

Reason #4: Resume Lacks Impact

What more can possibly be said about resumes, right? At this point, it feels like every career coach, hiring manager and recruiter has had their say. The think pieces, the hot takes, the endless streams of "dos and don'ts" on LinkedIn. You'd think the conversation would've died down by now, but it hasn't. Why? That's because the conversation still matters.

Resumes stir up a lot of emotions. Anxiety, confusion, frustration and sometimes even doubt. Because whether you like it or not, your resume often serves as the first impression. It's the face card of your professional story. It's the reason someone hits play and gives your career a second look or doesn't. So yeah, people are still looking for the secret sauce. Still hoping for that hidden formula that guarantees a callback. However, it's not just about strategy. It's about perception. That's why the resume conversation isn't going anywhere.

Resume anxiety is real. I've seen it in college students staring at a blank screen trying to write that first line. I've seen it in career changers, unsure of how to make their past make sense in a brand-new industry. I've seen it in seasoned executives who worry their experience reads as "overqualified" instead of accomplished. I've talked with stay-at-home parents returning to the workforce, worried a gap will close a door before they even knock. Now, we're layering on fears about artificial intelligence and applicant tracking systems like it's not hard enough already.

Here's something most people don't talk about. Even recruiters and hiring managers deal with their own version of resume stress. I've mentored many recruiters over the years who've shared how overwhelming it can be to sift through resumes under pressure, especially when expectations are high and time is tight. Some resumes look good on the surface but are full of exaggerations, AI terms or misrepresentations. Others are so overdesigned or jargon-heavy that the real story gets lost. Then there are the ones that just don't say anything at all. Just a long list of job titles with no heart, no impact, no proof of value.

So, after all the talk online, what exact purpose does the resume serve anyways? Look at it like this. Your resume is not just some boring, black-and-white list of jobs you've had. It's your hype reel. Your career movie trailer. That powerful two-minute preview that makes someone lean in and say, "Oh yeah, I need to see more."

Think about the last time you were sitting in the theater, popcorn in hand, the lights dim and the movie trailers started rolling. For a solid 15 to 20 minutes, you're not just watching, you're judging. You're analyzing. You're whispering to your friend, "Oh that one's fire. We gotta see that!" or "Yeah, I'll wait for that to hit streaming." You don't even need to see the full movie to know if it's worth your time. That's exactly how recruiters and hiring managers feel when they read your resume.

Your resume is supposed to spark curiosity. It's meant to showcase the best scenes and cuts from your professional life. The plot twists, the rising action, the standout performances. The moments that made you who you are in your career. You're not handing them the whole documentary. You're giving them a trailer so good, they can't wait to see the full feature. You're giving them a preview that gets you invited to the next phase, the interview.

Just like a dope movie trailer, your resume should have flow. It should have energy. It should build interest. That means leading with your strongest accomplishments, highlighting the wins that matter and cutting the fluff. You don't need every scene. You need the right ones. The ones that make the recruiter nudge their team member and say, "We need to call them in." So, whether you're early in your career or you've got years of footage to pull from, remember. You're not just telling your story, you're directing the trailer. The career hype reel.

7 Seconds to Showtime

If your resume is the hype reel of your career, then you've only got a few seconds to earn your standing ovation. According to the Ladders Eye Tracking Study back in 2018, recruiters only spend *7.4 seconds* on average reviewing a resume before deciding whether you make the cut. That's up from just 6 seconds during tougher times, like a recession. Why the rush? Because recruiters are swimming in a sea of applications, especially when there's a shaky job market. Their inboxes? Overflowing. Their time? Limited. So, your resume has to hit hard and hit fast the first time.

Let's break this down. In phase one of the study, recruiters were timed on how fast they reviewed resumes, without them knowing it. In phase two, eye-tracking technology was used to see exactly where their eyes landed to see what they noticed, and what they ignored. Here's the spoiler alert: resumes that were cluttered, hard to read, stuffed with keywords? They got the silent thumbs down. The ones that stood out? They had a clean layout, bold job titles, crisp bullet points that actually said something, and the fonts that didn't make you squint. Instead, they were simple, strong and straight to the point.

Now, the Ladders study we just talked about that said recruiters spend just 7.4 seconds scanning a resume, they weren't lying. I've lived it. I've been that recruiter with 200+ resumes staring back at me on a screen, deadlines breathing down my neck, hiring managers blowing up my inbox, and a whole list of roles that needed to be filled by yesterday. Seven seconds? Yeah, that sounds about right to me.

We're not being careless. We're being efficient. The volume is real, and when the stakes are high especially during layoffs, hiring freezes or post-pandemic surges, we have to move quick. That first scan is like a movie trailer. If it grabs me, if it hits just right, I'm sticking around. I'll watch the whole thing. I'll even replay it.

If your resume is clean, has a bold headline, bullet points that actually say something, and a layout that's easy on the eyes? You're getting a second look and focus in for much longer this go around. I might even pause my scroll, sit up in my chair, and say "Okay, let me see what this person is about."

Then there are the resumes that are… just okay. You didn't bomb, but you didn't shine either. And honestly? "Just okay" doesn't get callbacks. At best, you might land in the "maybe" list, but let me be real with you, that's recruiter code for "probably not." Not because you're not qualified, but because somebody else came stronger, faster and clearer with their story.

I've opened resumes with five different fonts, no structure, paragraphs longer than a Drake double album and job titles that read like someone just made them up on the spot. Even worse, I've had people apply with no resume at all. Just a name, maybe a LinkedIn link and prayers. That doesn't cut it. Not now. Not in this market.

All of this may seem overly critical, but I am obligated to be truthful. So, here's what I need you to understand. When a recruiter opens your resume, they're not just looking for what you've done. They're looking for whether you're worth calling. If your resume can make that decision easy, you win. That 7 seconds from the study? That's your shot. That's your trailer moment. That's when the recruiter either leans in or moves on. If it's good, you might earn 30 more seconds, then a full minute. Then a phone screen. Then an interview.

Your resume is your hype reel. Your highlight tape. Your "here's why I belong in this room" moment. So, make it count. The recruiters aren't your enemy, they're just busy. Give them a reason to slow down and take another look. Because when it hits? It hits.

Now let's flip the script. You know how you can tell within seconds if a movie is going to be fire or a flop? Same thing applies here. Your resume is your career movie teaser. It's your two-minute hype reel. No filler, no fluff. Just the highlights. The impact. The "this is why you need to see more."

This is your moment to pull the recruiter in like a must-watch trailer that gets a head nod and an elbow nudge. "This one?" That's the energy you want. So, think about the recruiter point of view to craft a resume that doesn't just sit in a stack, but stands out from. This isn't about hype for the sake of noise. It's about precision, clarity and impact that earns you a callback.

How To Crack the Code to an Impactful Resume

Now that you understand just how fast that first impression hits and how much weight your resume carries, let's get into what really makes that hype reel hit. Because once you've caught the recruiter's eye like a hot movie trailer in the first few seconds, the next step is keeping their attention long enough to want to watch the full feature. That's where intentionality comes in. Just like a movie trailer, it's not enough to just show up with scenes. You've got to show why people should care. The storyline matters. The impact matters, and the way you present it? That matters too.

This is not the time for fluff, filler or faking it. Your resume isn't just a list of jobs. It's your curated highlight reel. The scenes need to be strong, the dialogue clear and the impact undeniable.

This next part is for everybody who's ever stared at a blank Word doc, wondering how to talk about what they've done without sounding basic, boring or dull. It's for the people who've got the experience, but don't know how to package it in a way that pops. You've got receipts, now you just need help turning them into a highlight reel that recruiters want to press play on.

We're about to break down exactly how to do that—from keeping it real about your skillset, to showing receipts for your impact, to formatting your story like a professional. Let's move from basic to bold, and from good enough to standout. This next part is about how you make sure your hype reel actually lives up to the hype.

Be Truthful About Your Skillset

Let's start with the real talk. Your resume isn't the place to pose as someone you're not. That means you should be listing only the skills you actually possess, not the ones you think recruiters want to see. I've been on the other side of that screen too many times, reviewing resumes that listed every tool and tech skill under the sun, only for them to vanish once the interview comes. I would discover that they really didn't have them like they said they did.

Don't play yourself. That's a short-sighted strategy with long-term consequences.

Some job seekers even copy and paste the entire job description into their resume, thinking it'll help them play the system, but let me be clear about that. Keyword stuffing might get your resume past an applicant tracking system, maybe; or hit that AI algorithm really good, but it won't win over a recruiter who actually reads it. We notice, and once trust is broken, it's hard to recover.

Align your resume with the job description? Yes. Misrepresent your skills to do it? Absolutely not. Be real. The best thing you can bring to the table is the truth, well told. We'll unpack this even deeper in a later chapter.

Prioritize Your Impact

Nobody gets hired just for doing tasks. They get hired for making an impact. That's what your resume should show. Employers want to know what difference you made, not just what duties you had. When you write your resume, think in terms of impact.

Start by asking yourself two key questions:

1. **What did I innovate?** What did you create, launch or introduce that didn't exist before? It could be a new system, a client strategy, or even a fresh way to solve a recurring issue.
2. **What did I elevate?** What did you take from average to amazing? Did you optimize a process? Reignite a dormant relationship? Revamp a campaign?

Your answers should speak to how you made things better, more efficient, more profitable or more productive. Innovation and elevation are what make your hype reel worth watching.

Always Collect Your Wins

Here's a lesson I had to learn the hard way: don't wait until it's time to job hunt to think about your accomplishments. Keep track of them as they happen.

I had a mentor who once told me, "Bobby, if you don't collect your wins, nobody else will." That stuck with me. Ever since, I've kept a digital brag folder, a running list of moments I made impact, big or small. Whether it was saving the day in a pinch or getting props from leadership on a project, I wrote it down or filed it away.

You have to treat your wins like receipts. Because when it's time to refresh that resume or prepare for an interview, you'll have everything ready. Trust me, you don't want to be sitting at your laptop with relying solely on your memory. Keep those wins on deck.

Quantify Your Achievements

Now let's talk numbers. Your resume can tell a story, but the numbers make it real. That's your proof. Saying you "led a project" is fine, but saying you "led a cross-functional project that delivered a 15% growth in revenue in Q3"? Now that's how you do it.

When you quantify your impact, you give recruiters something tangible. We're talking time saved, revenue earned, improved customer satisfaction scores, retention increases, you name it. Think percentages, dollar amounts, ratios, timelines; these are the soundbites in the reel that stick. They give your trailer some box office appeal.

Effective Formatting

Last but definitely not least! How your resume looks matters just as much as what it says. Think of formatting like your professional posture. Stand tall. Be clear. No slouching.

Here's your resume formatting survival kit:

- **Keep it simple.** Fancy templates might look cute, but too many graphics or columns confuse ATS software and human eyes alike.
- **Use clean, readable fonts.** Between 10-12 point size. Don't go overboard trying to stand out with curly fonts or neon colors.
- **Be consistent.** Font sizes, bolding, bullet points. Everything should match. It's about flow and clarity.
- **Use action verbs in past tense** for previous roles, and present tense for your current one.
- **Trim the fat.** Don't list every job from the last 20 years. Stick to the last 7-10 years of your career. Summarize early career experiences collectively. Shoot for a two-page limit.
- **Strategically highlight.** Use bold and italics to draw attention to key sections, but don't overdo it.

A clean, well-organized resume says, "I care. I'm intentional. I respect your time." It's the kind of trailer that makes recruiters lean in and want more.

The Resume Reel: Section By Section

At this point in my career, I've lost count of how many resumes I've reviewed. Over the past 16 years, I've looked over several resumes a day, on the job and off the clock. That's not even including all the career sessions, freelance consultations and resume breakdowns I've done for people trying to get ahead. Reviewing resumes has been more than a duty, it's been a consistent part of my adult life.

While I used to shy away from calling myself an "expert," I've logged enough hours to claim that title with confidence. I've seen everything. Resumes packed with fluff, sections randomly arranged like a game of Tetris and layouts that leave you guessing what the person actually does for a living.

Let's be clear. The structure of your resume is not just about style, it's about strategy. The right section in the right place helps tell your career story in a clear, confident way. In this section, I'm not just going to show you what sections belong on your resume, I'm going to break down their real purpose, what to do, what to avoid and how to make each part work for you.

Whether you want to call this a crash course or a masterclass, we're about to walk through the anatomy of your resume from top to bottom. Let's build it the right way.

Contact Info: Keep It Clear, Keep It Clean

This section is your handshake. It should be clean, clear and easy to find.

Do:

- Use your **preferred name** and **add credentials** like MBA, RN, PhD, or PMP if earned.
- Include a *professional email* and *phone number*. Google Voice is a solid option for privacy.
- Add your **LinkedIn URL** and any **relevant links** (GitHub, portfolio, etc.).
- List your **city and state**. Zip code is optional. Note if you're open to relocating.

Do Not:

- Use **unprofessional nicknames** or **gimmicky monikers**. Keep your nickname in the group chat, not on your resume.
- Submit resumes with **no contact info** or a **cringey email**. Create a job-search-only one if needed.
- Add **irrelevant links** or a **headshot**. It takes up space and invites bias.
- Share your **full street address.** It's outdated and unnecessary.

Job Title: Control the Narrative

This is where you tell the recruiter exactly what role you're aiming for, no guessing games.

Do:

- **Insert a specific, targeted job title** like "Product Manager" or "Senior Data Analyst" that aligns with the position you're applying for.
- Use it to **boost your searchability**. This is the first keyword recruiters plug into search engines and ATS systems to find the top applicants.

Do Not:

- Include an **objective statement**. It's outdated, wordy and unnecessary. The Job Title section does the job with fewer words.
- Be vague or try to be "everything." Pick a lane and go that route clearly.

Summary: Set the Stage

This section is your setup. Your 15 second intro that if you were in-person, gets the recruiter ready for what's coming next.

Do:

- **Keep it concise.** Aim for 4-5 sentences max. Hit that sweet spot between not enough and way too much.

- **Highlight your impact.** Focus on your top 2–3 skills relevant to the role, years of experience, biggest accomplishments and relevant certifications.
- **Tailor it to the role you're pursuing.** Think of this as a quick preview of the value you bring.

Do Not:

- Turn it into a **cover letter** or a **life story.** Leave out personal backstories, job search struggles or hobbies.
- **Overdo the adjectives.** You don't need a string of "results-driven, passionate, motivated…" back-to-back. Let your experience speak louder than the fluff.
- Summarize what you "hope to do."

Skills: What You Really Bring to the Table

The Skills section is where you highlight what you can actually do. It should reinforce your strengths and give the recruiter a quick snapshot of your capabilities. No guesswork required.

Do:

- **Tell the truth.** Only include skills you can confidently speak to and demonstrate.
- **Be specific.** Don't just say "coding" or "communication." Instead, say "JavaScript, Python" or "executive-level stakeholder presentations."
- **Include both technical and business skills.** Think about tools, platforms and competencies that are relevant to the job and industry.

- **Keep it current.** Only list skills that are in-demand and that you've used recently.

Do Not:

- **Fake it.** Listing tools or methods you barely touched will catch up with you in the interview. Or even worse on the job.
- **Be too vague.** General terms like "teamwork" or "problem-solving" don't help much unless they're backed up by context elsewhere.
- **List outdated or irrelevant skills.** Leave out tools that are obsolete or unrelated to the role you're targeting.

Work Experience: The Main Event

This is the heartbeat of your resume. It's where you show what you've done, who you've done it for and most importantly what kind of impact you've made.

Do:

- **Keep it relevant.** Use industry-specific language and keywords to describe your experience.
- **List in reverse chronological order.** Start with your current or most recent job and work backwards.
- **Be intentional with the bullet points.** Quantify and qualify results when possible.
    - Tailor content to prioritize the most recent roles.
    - Recent roles (last 7 years): 4–6 impactful bullet points.

- o Older roles (8–10 years ago): 2–4 impactful bullet points.
- o Early career (10+ years): 1–2 bullet points

Do Not:

- **Overload with details.** You're not writing a novel. Prioritize what matters.
- **Repeat the job description.** Focus on your impact, not just what the job required.
- **Hold on to irrelevant roles.** If the job was over 10 years ago and unrelated, it's okay to leave it off.

Here's an example of an impactful bullet point: *"Led a cross-functional team to launch a new product line, resulting in $2.5M in revenue within the first six months."* Bottom line. This section should read like a highlight reel, not a play-by-play.

Education: The Credentials Check

This is where you show the formal knowledge and training behind your skill set. Whether it's degrees, certifications or bootcamps, this section tells the recruiter you've got the foundation to back up your experience.

Do:

- **Include the essentials.** School name, degrees earned, major/minor and honors like Dean's List, Cum Laude if you have them.

- **Add certifications.** Especially if they're required or highly relevant to the role. List the issuing organization and completion date.
- **Lead with education** if you're early in your career. However, if you've been working for several years, it can follow your work experience.

Do Not:

- **Stretch the truth.** If you're still in school, list your expected graduation date. If you didn't finish, you can mention the number of credit hours earned.
- **Overload with extras.** Keep it clean and relevant. Leave hobbies, unrelated clubs or outdated courses off unless they directly support your current goals.

Remember, your resume, it's not just a document. It's your hype reel. The movie trailer of your career. It's the first impression before the feature film; and just like any great trailer, it has one job; to make the audience want more.

The sections we walked through? They're not random bullet points or buzzword. They're your highlight scenes. The parts that make people sit up, pay attention and say, "Now that's somebody I need to know more about." Your contact info? That's your title screen. Your job title and summary? That's your opening scene. Your skills and experience? That's the action montage. Your education? That's the closing credits that reminds people this wasn't luck. It's been earned.

Too many times, I've seen bright, talented people let the wrong version of their story get told or worse, but now you've got the script. You've got the lens. You know how to frame it. When the right person presses play, your resume should leave them with no doubt about who you are, qualified and ready for more.

So, don't undersell the trailer to your career. If your resume doesn't hype you up, it's time to reshoot the scenes. Rewrite the script. Recut the footage. It isn't the end. It's just the preview of something legendary.

Chapter 5

Pre-Interview Power Moves
Get in Position

Reason #5: Lack Of Preparation & Readiness

I've been in the recruiting game for well over a decade. Various roles in different industries, award-winning hiring strategies, and countless phone screens under my belt. And if there's one thing that still makes me shake my head, it's this; candidates who land the interview, hop on the call, and aren't ready. I'm not talking about nerves. I mean people who don't know what the role is, can't speak on the company, or worse, forgot they applied. That's not just disappointing, it's a missed opportunity. I've seen talent with real potential trip over the basics simply because they didn't take time to prepare.

Now look, if a recruiter hits you with a cold call out the blue. Fair enough. You weren't expecting it; and honestly, they probably aren't having a lot of expectation of you to be prepped either. However, when you applied, and you chose the time to speak? That's your moment, and how you show up matters. Preparation isn't a chore; it's a power move. It sets the tone, frames the conversation and lets the recruiter know you didn't just show up, you came to get the job. When you've done your homework, it's obvious. The conversation flows smoother. The energy is high, and suddenly, you're not just another name on a list, you're the one they remember.

Picture this: it's the end of the year, and I'm deep in the recruiting trenches. My day was stacked with back-to-back phone screens, endless LinkedIn sourcing sessions and intake calls with hiring managers who were practically pacing the floor, anxiously trying to get tech talent in the door before year-end. The holiday vibes were heavy. My living room was calling, the sweet smell of cookies lingered from the kitchen and I had plans to unwind with Christmas movies and my family later that evening.

Just as I was about to head back into my home office for one last interview call, my girlfriend at the time popped out of the kitchen wearing her cute Santa hat, holding a warm, sugar cookie fresh from the oven. "Babe, try one," she said with a playful smile, gently rubbing my shoulder. She kissed me on the cheek, slid the cookie into my mouth like a little holiday gift, then darted back downstairs before I could even respond. It was one of those small, perfect moments, sweet, familiar, grounding. It was almost like she knew I needed that after a long hard recruiting day.

I was tired. The kind of tired that creeps in when your brain is running on coffee, your calendar's been hijacked and all you really want is a break. Still, I've always prided myself on being a candidate advocate, so I took a sip of hot chocolate, took a breath and dialed in. Let me tell you, what happened next, flipped my whole mood.

This candidate showed up and they showed out. Their qualifications were solid, no doubt, but that wasn't what made the moment memorable. It was their energy. Their prep work. Their hunger. From the second we started talking, I could feel it. This person had done their homework. They weren't just familiar with the job, they understood the business, the product and the mission. Their questions weren't generic. They were thoughtful, personal, specific.

Then came the part that really caught me off guard. They asked about me. Not on a surface level, "So, what's your role?" kind of way, but in a way that showed they were connecting the dots between the people behind the process. This candidate was also connecting with me as well. They made the conversation feel like a two-way street; and right there, in the middle of my last screen before holiday break, I realized I wasn't just talking to another candidate. I was talking to someone who came prepared to make an impact.

Fast forward a few weeks, guess who became my very first hire of the new year? That experience wasn't just a feel-good moment. It was a real-time reminder that preparation is your power play. It's not just about knowing the job description or practicing your pitch.

It's about showing up with intentionality, curiosity and clarity. When you do, you don't just interview. You resonate.

Memorable for All the Right Reasons

I've interviewed thousands of candidates over the course of my career across all industries, backgrounds and career levels. From interns fresh out of college to very experienced C-Suite leaders, I've seen the full spectrum. I've sat on both sides of the table. As a recruiter, yes, but also as a candidate applying for roles, being courted for new opportunities and navigating interviews myself. That dual perspective taught me something powerful that the interview is never just a formality. It's a moment, a chance to rise to the occasion, to make people remember you not just as a name on a resume, but as a presence.

Some candidates do just that. They turn the conversation into a moment. I've seen it firsthand. There are candidates I'll never forget, not because the candidate had the perfect background, but because of how they showed up. They didn't just show me their qualifications. They showed me who they were, what they stood for and how they thought.

Like the candidate one time who asked such sharp, strategic questions that the hiring manager completely reimagined the role and ended up creating a senior-level leadership position tailored specifically for them. Or the one I had who walked in with a mini presentation deck they built themselves, not because anyone told them to, but because they cared enough to connect their own story to our company values. That kind of preparation? That kind of creativity? It's undeniable.

Even when I was on the other side as a candidate, I operated with that same mindset. If I'm getting the opportunity to be in the room, I'm going to leave something behind, not just a resume, but a lasting impression.

Now, I want to show you exactly what those top-tier candidates did. The ones who stood out and shifted the room. The ones who turned the interview into a feature presentation where they were the main character. Here are the common traits they shared:

- They pulled a few key bullets from the job description and connected them directly to their key experiences and skills. No fluff; just alignment.
- Their answers were clear, tight and easy to follow. They didn't ramble; they delivered.
- They were confident, but grounded. They knew their value, but also knew they didn't know everything. That balance was impactful.
- They understood who their audience was. They did their homework, not just on the company, but on the people in the room. They anticipated what would matter most to us.
- They did not allow tough questions rattle them. They stayed poised. No flinching, no folding.
- Their non-verbal communication matched the energy. The eye contact, posture, the occasional smile. They were present.

- Their questions weren't generic. They asked things that made us think and made the conversation better.
- They connected their values to ours and did it in a way that felt real, not rehearsed.
- They went beyond the words. Some built short presentations, shared mock projects or brought in thoughtful examples of their work. It wasn't extra, it was effective.

The best candidates I've ever witnessed weren't always the flashiest, the most extroverted or the most brilliant. What set them apart, what made them truly memorable was the work they put in before the interview even began.

They came prepared. Not just with facts about the company or an overly rehearsed elevator pitch, but with intention. They had studied the role, reflected on their own experience and thought critically about how they could add value and connect the dots. They weren't winging it. They came ready to connect with the interviewer, with the mission and with the opportunity itself.

That kind of preparation is powerful. It shows respect for the process, for the people involved and for themselves. It says, "I didn't just show up. I showed up ready."

When you show up ready, you shift the energy in the room. You make it easy for decision-makers to see you not just as a candidate, but as the right one.

So, as you keep moving through this journey, remember what happens before the interview often determines what happens after it. The preparation you do now? That's the real power move.

How To Crack the Code to Preparation & Readiness

The best candidates? They clock in early by putting in the work before the interview ever starts; and trust me, it shows. The way they spoke, the way they asked questions, the confidence they carried. It all pointed back to one thing, preparation.

It's amazing how just a little pre-interview research can flip the entire energy of a conversation. Not only does it leave a lasting impression on the recruiter or hiring manager, but it fuels something within you too, confidence. It's the kind of confidence that doesn't just help you answer questions. It helps you seize the moment.

And that's what this part of the journey is really about owning your moment. It's not just about being qualified. It's about making it undeniable that you're the one they've been looking for. When you prepare, you don't just sound better, you feel better. Your posture changes. Your tone hits different. You show up sharp, informed, and ready to tackle anything. That kind of energy is contagious and it's memorable.

Before you hop on that next Zoom call or walk into the next lobby with your folder in hand, take a moment. Breathe. Get focused. And make sure you've checked the right boxes.

Here are a few game-changing pre-interview moves that will help you get in position and walk into the room like you already belong there.

Industry Intel: Do Your Homework Like a Pro

One of the most underrated power moves you can make before an interview is doing your homework. And I'm not talking about just skimming the company website 10 minutes before the call. I mean locking in and gathering real, meaningful information that helps you show up sharp, confident, and conversation ready.

The best candidates I've seen over the years didn't just wing it. They took time to dig a little deeper, and it paid off.

Start by checking out recent news articles. Maybe the company just launched a new product, acquired a smaller firm, or their CEO rang the Opening Bell on the New York Stock Exchange. That kind of detail can be a perfect icebreaker or a thoughtful way to frame your questions during the interview.

Don't stop there. Dive into their LinkedIn page and explore beyond the basics. Get a feel for how big the company is, what industry conversations they're part of, and what their core values actually mean in practice. A little recon here can spark some great talking points and more importantly, shows that you care enough to come prepared.

Now let's go a little deeper:

- **Interviewing at a finance firm?** Skim through their quarterly earnings or recent investor call recaps to get a sense of how the business is performing.
- **Going after a tech role?** See what innovations or patents they're cooking up, or how they're using AI, automation, or cloud solutions to scale.
- **Got a shot with a civil engineering firm?** Look into what roadway or infrastructure projects they're tackling in your region. Especially ones funded through recent federal or local grants.

Whatever the industry, make it your business to know their business.

Find Common Ground: Build the Bridge before the Conversation Starts

Do your homework on the interviewer, not just the company.

Before you even step into the interview, whether that's on Zoom or in person. Take a few minutes to study who's on the other side of the table. Pull up their LinkedIn profile. This isn't just about being nosy. It's about being intentional.

Did you go to the same school? Volunteer for a similar cause? Maybe you both care deeply about diversity in tech. These small commonalities can open big doors. They turn interviews from stiff Q&A sessions into real conversations between two people who just get each other. And trust me, when a hiring manager feels that it makes a lasting impression.

Take it a step further. Look at their activity section on LinkedIn. What are they posting, sharing, or commenting on? Are they speaking at events, mentoring others, advocating for something? This gives you a window into what they value. When you understand what your interviewer values, you walk into that room equipped to speak their language.

It's not about trying to impress. It's about trying to connect, because when you build that bridge early, you're no longer just another name on the calendar. You become memorable. Relatable. Someone they could see on the team.

Know Your Role: Then Go Deeper

There's nothing more frustrating for a recruiter than hopping on a call with a candidate who doesn't know the basics about the job they applied for. We're not talking about memorizing the entire job posting word for word, but knowing the essentials is a bare minimum expectation. It's like showing up to a first date and forgetting the person's name. Sure, you might recover, but it's an uphill battle.

One of the easiest and most impactful things you can do before an interview is know the role. Not in theory. Not vaguely, but clearly. What's the job title? Where's it located? What are the core responsibilities? What technical or digital skills are required? What level of education or experience do they want? You don't need to have it all down to a science, but you should be able to explain the basics back in your own words and speak to how your background connects.

Getting these essentials down helps in two major ways. First, it sets the tone that you're prepared and serious about the opportunity. Second, it frees up mental space for you to dig deeper during the interview. You can spend your time having thoughtful, next-level conversations instead of wasting it asking questions that could've been answered with a five-minute skim of the job post.

Now, look I get it. Job hunting is no joke. Between juggling multiple interviews, remembering which recruiter said what, and trying to keep your hopes up without burning out, it's a lot. That's why staying organized isn't just helpful, it's essential. My advice? Start a job tracker. It doesn't have to be fancy. Whether it's a spreadsheet in Excel, a Google Doc or just a running list in your Notes app, create a place to log the roles you're applying for. Include company names, job titles, dates you applied, who you've spoken with and upcoming interview times.

Flip the Script: Interview Them

Too many job seekers walk into interviews feeling like they're at the mercy of the employer, but here's the truth. The interview isn't just for them to evaluate you. It's for you to evaluate them as well. It's your moment too. You're not just applying to fill a seat, you're deciding whether this seat fits your purpose and your progression.

One of the most powerful things you can do is flip the script. Come to the interview prepared to interview the interviewers. I've seen this mindset shift change the entire tone of a conversation. The best candidates I've ever spoken to didn't just answer questions; they asked them with purpose, curiosity and clarity. It didn't just impress me, it showed me that they were confident in their value and clear about what they wanted in return.

Think of it like this. If you're going to show up as the main character in your interview, then this is your scene to take some creative control. You have every right to ask meaningful questions that help you decide if this is the right script, cast and stage for you.

That said, be mindful of what you ask. There's a line between engaging and invasive. Don't waste your moment on surface level questions that could've been answered in the job description or by glancing at the company's homepage. And definitely don't grill the interviewer like you're holding a grudge. The goal isn't to catch them off guard; it's to create connection and clarity.

Instead, ask the kind of questions that go beneath the surface— questions that help you gauge the culture, the leadership style, the challenges you'd be stepping into and the way success is measured. This shows that you're not just hungry for a paycheck—you're looking for alignment, growth and the right environment to thrive in.

Here are a few curated, high-impact questions you might consider walking into your next interview with:

- *What has led to the availability of this position?*
- *Could you outline the typical career progression for a role like this?*
- *As my potential manager, can you share with me how you typically lead and oversee the team I might join?*

- *Which of the company's core values resonate the most with you and your team and why?*
- *What are the primary challenges currently being faced by the team?*
- *If I were to start this job tomorrow, what's the first big problem you would want me to take care of?*
- *Can you describe the onboarding process for new hires?*
- *Could you provide insights into the team I'll directly work with and the cross-functional teams I'll collaborate with?*
- *If I were to join, what would be the most pivotal task to accomplish within the first 90 days of this role?*
- *Other than what's outlined in the job description, could you elaborate on additional tools and resources that will be provided to support the essential job duties?*
- *What is something that is not in the job description, but is crucial for success in this role?*
- *How is success defined and what metrics are used to measure performance in this position?*
- *What steps should I anticipate in the upcoming interview process, and how would you suggest I best prepare for them?*
- *Are there any specific concerns or reservations about how I might fit into this role?*

These types of questions aren't about filling in time. They set the tone. They show you came with purpose. They turn the interview into a two-way dialogue where both sides are discovering if this is the right fit.

Let's talk facts. With more and more CEOs rolling out return-to-office mandates in 2024, it's safe to say the era of fully remote work is slowly fading off into the rearview. While remote opportunities still exist, they're becoming increasingly scarce and hybrid work models where you're expected to be in the office a few days a week are becoming the new norm.

And with that shift, comes something many candidates haven't had to think about in a minute; and that's the in-person interview.

Yep, the days of hopping on back-to-back video calls in your pajama bottoms and a crisp button up are starting to fade, and in-person interviews are back in rotation. I've heard from plenty of job seekers who admit they haven't had to do one of these in years and to be real, it shows. Virtual interviews are still a vital skill, no doubt; but now, it's time to also dust off your in-person game and show up like you belong in the room.

Being invited to an on-site interview is more than just a formality; it's a chance to bring your presence, energy and professionalism to life. This is where you make the strongest impression, not just through your answers, but through your energy, your body language and your overall approach. When you get that call to come in, don't panic, get prepared. Here's how to walk in confident, centered and ready to leave a mark.

Dress for the Industry, Not Just the Interview

Every job interview doesn't call for a stiff suit and tie or a perfectly pressed power dress. One of the biggest mistakes candidates make when prepping for in-person interviews is assuming there's a one size fits all approach to dressing the part. That couldn't be further from the truth. Different industries have different cultures, and what you wear should match the vibe of where you're going.

I've recruited across the board, from tech, finance, manufacturing, you name it; and trust me, what's appropriate in one space can look completely out of place in another.

If you're heading into an interview at a traditional corporate office like banking, legal or Fortune 500 firms, go full business professional. That means a dark suit, tie and clean white shirt if you're masculine presenting, or a tailored dress or blazer/slacks combo with if you're going for a more feminine look. C-suite executives roam those hallways, and your outfit should reflect that level of formality.

However, if you're walking into a tech startup, creative agency or a product design firm, you'll want to pivot. Keep the full business suit at home and lean into smart casual. A blazer with clean dark jeans or chinos, a nice sweater or blouse and some clean shoes or flats that still say, "I came to play, but I'm not trying too hard" will do the trick.

Now, if the interview is happening in a warehouse, plant or manufacturing environment, business casual takes on a whole new look. Think polished, but practical. A clean polo or button-down shirt, tidy dark jeans (no holes) and close-toed shoes are the move. Safety and comfort matter here, but that doesn't mean you shouldn't still look the part.

The Interview Starts in the Parking Lot and Ends When You Leave It

Most people think the interview starts when they sit down across from the hiring manager, but let me let you in on a little secret that many job seekers overlook. The interview actually starts as soon as you pull onto company property, and it doesn't officially end until you've pulled off it. That means from the moment your front tire touches that parking lot, you're on stage.

Arriving about 15 minutes early gives you time to breathe, center yourself and avoid the stress of racing into the building. Trust me, nothing says "unprepared" like peeling into the parking lot late, hopping out the car and scrambling to find the entrance. While it might seem small, turn your music down or better yet, off before you turn in. I remember one time back in the day, I had Meek Mill's *Dreams & Nightmares* on repeat, full blast, the whole drive down Glenwood Avenue in Raleigh. It was my hype anthem before a big interview, but as I turned the corner toward the building, I turned it off. Why? Because as much as I needed to get in the zone, I also knew how to read the moment. I had awareness. I read the room before I even got in it. I needed to walk in poised, calm and focused. (And yes, I got that job.)

When the interview wraps up, you're still being evaluated. I've seen candidates undo all the great impressions they made in the room just by what they did in the last five minutes. I've watched someone throw trash on the ground outside the office. I've heard stories of near misses in the parking lot with employees walking to their cars as a candidate sped off. That kind of behavior stays with people. Companies don't just want someone who can do the job, they want someone they won't regret inviting into their workplace culture.

So, remember, once you pull in, you're being seen; and once you drive off, then it's over.

Be Kind to Everyone. No Exceptions

Here's a golden rule that often gets overlooked. Kindness isn't just reserved for the hiring manager. The moment you step foot on company property, every interaction becomes part of your interview, whether you realize it or not.

Be courteous to everyone you encounter. This includes the parking attendant, the receptionist at the front desk, the janitorial crew, the café staff, the security guard, even the employee you briefly pass in the hallway. These moments matter more than you might think. Word travels fast in a workplace, and yes, I've seen hiring managers and recruiters casually ask, *"Hey, what did you think of that candidate?"* to someone who wasn't even on the interview panel.

Here's a reminder worth repeating. Regardless of title or status, these individuals are already employed at the company you're hoping to join. That alone deserves your respect. How you treat people when you think they "don't matter" says a lot about your character. Trust me, it will make its way back to the decision makers.

Don't Come to the Interview Empty-Handed

If you want to be taken seriously as a candidate, how you show up matters. One of the simplest ways to signal that you're polished and prepared is to walk in with a clean, professional looking notepad or leather padfolio and a good pen. You don't have to break the bank, just something that says, "I didn't just roll out of bed and show up."

Additionally, bring a few extra copies of your resume. Even if the interview is scheduled with a full panel, people still appreciate having a printed copy in hand. It's a professional gesture that never goes out of style. if you've got examples of your work like a portfolio, case study or project deck, bring those too. Real, tangible examples of your talent leave an impression that words alone can't.

Also, don't just carry the padfolio to look the part; use it. Take notes throughout the conversation. Not only does this show that you're locked in and actively listening, it also allows you to capture key gems from the discussion. It could be a project the team is excited about, a new initiative that aligns with your passions or details about the role's growth potential. These are the types of nuggets that help you ask better follow up questions, tailor your thank you note and evaluate deeper if the opportunity truly fits you.

In closing, if your resume is the hype reel, then the interview is the feature presentation where the audience finally gets to see what you're really about; and just like any great performance, what happens behind the scenes is just as important as what happens in the spotlight.

Preparation is getting you in position. It's how you set the tone before you even say a word. From the moment your car hits the lot to the second those doors close behind you, you're leaving an impression. Every eye contact, every handshake, every thoughtful question is a frame in the film you're directing.

The truth is that the best candidates I've ever seen weren't just lucky or smooth talkers, they did the work ahead of time. They researched, anticipated and aligned their story with the company's values. As a result, they didn't just answer questions, they created moments.

This chapter isn't about telling you how to ace an interview just for the sake of it. It's about owning your space before you walk into that room. It's about remembering that preparation isn't just a task, but a form of self-respect.

So, the next time you step into an interview, don't just go in hoping for the best. Go in knowing you've already done the work to get in position. Lights, camera, ready? Because the show is yours now.

Chapter 6

The Art of Storytelling
Say It Like You Mean It

Reason #6: Didn't Clearly Communicate Your Value

L et me take you behind the scenes for a moment. As a recruiter who's combed through thousands of resumes over the years across tech and non-tech, from entry-level to the executive suite. I've seen some resumes that read like box-office blockbusters. We're talking powerful metrics, bold impact and polished language that practically jumps off the page. Maybe they saved a company $1.2 million. Maybe they drove user traffic through the roof. The kind of stuff that makes a hiring manager perk up like, *"Okay, now we're talkin."* Then the interview rolls around.

Suddenly, that same candidate, the one who seemed like the next big thing is stumbling over their words, struggling to connect the dots, unsure how to explain the "how" behind the "wow." And just like that, the momentum fizzles. The movie doesn't live up to the once hyped trailer. Sound familiar?

This is more common than people realize. Plenty of candidates know how to write the part, but can't seem to say the part when it matters most. They freeze. They ramble. They fumble. And listen, I get it. Interviews are high pressure situations, but that's exactly why being able to clearly and confidently articulate your story is a game changing skill, especially in today's world, where storytelling is everything.

Here's the truth, if your resume is the trailer, your interview is the full-length feature. It's your time to prove that the hype is real.

Throughout your job search, you'll likely encounter three main types of interviews: the recruiter screen (the vibe check), the technical or skill-based assessment (the "show me what you got") and the behavioral interview (the "show me who you are"). They might look a little different depending on the industry or company, but the common thread is that no matter what industry, being able to tell your own career story is your most powerful tool.

That last one, that behavioral interview, is what often separates the candidates who look good on paper from the ones who truly leave a mark, because it's not just about what you did; it's about how you explain it, how you connect the dots, how you make them feel like they just met someone they need on their team.

For employers, behavioral interviews serve a double purpose. First, they offer a chance to dig deeper into the highlights on your resume and get to the behind-the-scenes footage, not just the headline. Second, they're watching to see how you show up as a communicator. Can you break things down clearly? Can you connect with different kinds of people? Can you tell your story in a way that feels real, confident and grounded?

That's what this chapter is all about, learning how to do just that.

So, if you've ever left an interview feeling like you didn't really say what you meant to, or you froze when it was time to shine, don't worry. You're not alone. Let's get you in the zone to not just tell your story, but to own it.

People Remember Stories, Not Buzzwords

When it comes to interviews, buzzwords are everywhere. Everyone's a "strategic thinker," a "strong communicator" or a "results-driven professional." After interviewing thousands of candidates, I can tell you with confidence, what sticks with interviewers isn't the jargon, it's the story.

Effective communication is non-negotiable. No matter what industry you're in or what level you're applying for, your ability to clearly communicate your value is what opens doors and keeps them open. As a Recruiting Leader, I've not only coached candidates through interviews, but I've also played the role of hiring manager myself, building high-performing teams of my own. That experience gave me firsthand insight into what hiring managers are really listening for, and it isn't fluff, it's substance.

If you've made it to the interview stage, that already means there's interest, but the moment you step into that room or log onto that Zoom, the interview becomes an audition. The hiring manager isn't just evaluating your resume bullet points; they're picturing you delivering high-stakes presentations, collaborating with peers, jumping into a fire drill or explaining your strategy to a senior leader. They're asking themselves, can this person communicate in a way that moves the team forward?

That's why storytelling matters. I've seen countless candidates come alive when they weave their experiences into powerful mini stories that show (not just tell) the value they bring. Stories give context. They showcase problem-solving. They prove you understand the work, and more than anything else, stories are what people remember.

Here's the truth. The buzzwords might help you sound prepared, but storytelling is what helps interviewers see you in the role; that's what makes all the difference.

Most interview processes follow a similar structure, no matter the company or industry. You'll typically face an initial recruiter screen, a technical assessment and a behavioral based interview. While all three stages matter, it's that behavioral-based interview where your storytelling and communication skills really get tested. This is where the interviewer wants to know how you handled real situations in your career, your thought process, what actions you took and what came out of it.

The Society of Human Resources Management (SHRM) defines Behavioral-Based Interviewing as "a technique which focuses on a candidate's past experiences, behaviors, knowledge, skills and abilities by asking the candidate to provide specific examples of when they have demonstrated certain behaviors or skills in the past as a means of predicting future behavior and performance."

Alright so we've made it clear. Buzzwords might get you in the room, but stories are what get you remembered. Real talk? Hiring managers don't stay up at night replaying your "strategic thinker with excellent communication skills" line, but they will remember how you broke down that messy project you inherited and turned it into a win.

Here's the thing, knowing you've got a good story and actually telling it in a way that lands. That's a whole different skill set. You need structure. You need sauce. You need delivery; and most of all, you need a method that keeps you from rambling like you're on the back porch with your cousin at the cookout.

That's where the STAR Method comes in. It's the blueprint. A go-to formula that helps you package your wins in a way that's clear, concise and clutch under pressure. Now, if you've ever been told to "use the STAR method" in interviews, but never got the how or why behind it, don't worry. I got you.

Development Dimensions International (DDI), a groundbreaking leadership consulting firm that's been ahead of the game for decades, created the STAR Interviewing Method back in 1974. DDI introduced STAR as a simple, but powerful framework to help candidates communicate more effectively in interviews. Since then, it's been the gold standard.

I've coached countless candidates from entry level to executive, using this method; and when it's used right? It's incredibly effective.

Here's how it breaks down:

- **S = Situation**
  - Set the stage. What was going on? What challenge were you facing?
- **T = Task**
  - What was your role? What were you responsible for doing?
- **A = Action**
  - What steps did you take to solve the issue or move things forward?
- **R = Result**
  - What was the outcome? What changed or improved because of your actions?

Simple. Clear. Impactful. And when done well, your STAR stories do more than answer a question they build trust, prove value, and leave a lasting impression. So, as you prepare for your next interview, remember, that buzzwords fade, but a great story? That's what gets remembered.

How to Crack the Code to
Telling a Compelling Narrative

Now that we've unpacked the STAR Method, let me show you how I didn't just talk about it, I lived it. This isn't some hypothetical story from a career blog. This is from my journey. A real achievement that helped me land my second leadership-level role in Talent Acquisition; and yes, that same win is still posted proudly on my resume to this day. No fluff. No filler. Just straight facts.

This wasn't your average "couple of questions and we'll be in touch" interview. Nope, this was a marathon. Four different interviewers, each assigned to drill me on a different core value tied to the company's culture. Collaboration. Innovation. Ownership. Resilience. Each interviewer came with four deep behavioral-based questions, and none of them were softball. I knew I had to come correct.

So, for two straight days, I locked in and went full prep mode. I did a digital dash across LinkedIn, studying every interviewer's background like game film. I looked at their roles, what teams they led, what they posted, what they liked, even what projects they celebrated. That told me everything I needed to know. What they valued, what they were likely to ask, and how I needed to respond.

I made a playbook, like we used to do back in my college basketball days. Preparation and discipline were everything. It's what drove us to be champions. You don't just show up hoping for the best, you prepare with intention, you run the drills and when game day hits, you already know the plays. This was no different here. I had responses queued up. If they hit me with a question on navigating change, I had the perfect story. If they skipped past it, I had three other lanes ready to run through. It was an interviewing card game, and I was two moves ahead.

Right in the middle of all this preparation, I got a warm phone call from my big sister. She didn't have to say much, just wished me luck and reminded me, "You've already done the work. Now just go be you." That little boost was the fuel I didn't know I needed.

There were multiple questions and interviewers that day, but there was one interviewer I knew I had to impress. That was VP of Talent Acquisition. The buck stopped with him. He was the Final Boss of this entire interview process, the one with the final say. What he said was going to go. I'm sure he had already sized me up, but little did he know. I had already done the same. I knew the angle he was coming at, and I had two big Draw 4s ready to slam down that would get me to Uno, plus another response in my pocket to seal the game if he wanted to go another direction.

His Question:

"Bobby, please share a project or initiative you led to discover candidates and describe its impact on the team and stakeholders?"

My Response:

S: Situation

"Our technical recruiting team faced a challenge with specific diversity hiring metrics for a software engineering recruitment campaign. The third-party diversity job board had a low number of applicants, which caused a setback in our efforts."

T: Task

"As the lead and most senior level technical recruiter on the team, I recognized the need to expand our efforts beyond traditional methods to better engage with diverse talent in software engineering. I spearheaded the creation of a virtual event. It was a fireside chat centered around a topic that piqued the interest of diverse software engineers. The event featured a panel of company leaders, tailored specifically to resonate with software engineers who fit our criteria for diverse hires."

A: Action

"I assembled a panel from different levels of management within the division by giving them a high-level presentation on the value added. I worked with a project manager to provide the virtual platform best suitable for an event that would include a moderator, panelist, and Q&A features. In addition to, I got buy in from the other recruiters making it fun and competitive for prizes to those that would get the most hires from the event and the most sourced candidates to attend. I established metrics as well with approval from my manager to make sure they aligned with our overall goal.

With our target audience in mind, I motivated the team not only to engage candidates already in the recruitment process but also to actively generate fresh prospects through various outbound methods."

R: Result

"Our goal was to secure 40 RSVPs, considering an anticipated 40% drop-off rate for actual attendees, and achieve a minimum of 1 hire within 45 days. We exceeded our goals by attaining 47 RSVPs and achieving 3 hires within 43 days, which means we not only surpassed our RSVP and hire targets but also outpaced our time-to-fill goal, making the initiative a success for our broader team metrics."

As I finished my response, I watched him closely. The VP of Talent Acquisition, the Final Boss in this entire interview process. He had held his poker face tight the whole time, barely giving an inch, but in that moment, I caught it. A slight smirk of approval. Nothing exaggerated, nothing forced. Just enough to say, "Okay… you got it."

That's when I knew I had landed the moment I'd been preparing for. All the mental reps, the LinkedIn deep-dives, the sleepless nights playing out interview scenarios in my head. They weren't just practice. They were the game plan; and it worked.

The very next day, I was on the phone negotiating my offer. Two weeks later, I walked through the doors of my new company, stepping into my second leadership-level role in Talent Acquisition. It felt good, not just because I won the job, but because I earned it by showing up prepared, confident and fully myself.

Yes, I beat the interview game that day, but the truth is, so did he. The company didn't just fill a role. They found the right person to lead and deliver. That's the beauty of a great interview. When it's done right, everybody wins.

Chapter 7

In the Hot Seat
Thriving When Tested

Reason #7: Inability To Showcase Your Skills

Alright picture this. You're in the interview. Not just talking about what you can do but being asked to prove it on the spot. Everything shifts. It's no longer just conversation. It's a live demonstration. This is the moment where the resume takes a backseat, and your real skills have to show up and show out. It's like being in the fourth quarter of a tied-up playoff game, center stage at the BET Awards or that last round in a rap battle where the crown's on the line. The lights are bright, the stakes are high and all eyes are on you. You're in the hot seat now.

This phase of the interview is what we call the Skills Assessment. Sometimes it's a case study. Sometimes it's a presentation. Sometimes it's a technical test, a role play or a series of job-related scenarios. Whatever form it takes, one thing is guaranteed, it's the part of the process where you've got to walk it like you've been talking it.

I've seen it play out hundreds of times as a recruiter and I've been through it myself. Whether you're trying to get into a new company or level up to a leadership role, you're going to hit that moment where preparation meets pressure. Where theory meets execution. Where confidence meets the challenge. The higher you climb, the more often you'll find yourself tested, watched and evaluated for how you respond under fire. Not just for what you say you know, but for what you can show.

Let me share with you some moments when I was in that exact seat. The lights were on, the pressure was real, and what I did next made all the difference...

Thriving when tested isn't just something that shows up in the interview room. It shows up everywhere. It's in the defining moments that shape our careers, our confidence and our credibility. I've lived it firsthand, in rooms with spotlights, on hardwood floors, on stages and in corporate boardrooms. Whether it was the fourth quarter or the final round, the ability to perform under pressure has always been there.

Let me take it all the way back to high school. I wasn't just another player. I was one of the top basketball prep stars in the state of North Carolina. I'm talking sold out gymnasiums, Friday night lights indoors, the roar of the crowd, the haters yelling from the stands and that defender in my face trying to throw me off my game. We're down by one, and there's just a few seconds left on the clock. I've got the ball. College scouts and coaches are in the crowd watching closely, wanting to see for themselves if the kid they kept seeing in the high school sports section of the paper was really who they say he is. I had prepared for this moment. All those drills, the late practices, the hours in the gym. It all led to this. Two dribbles, crossover, step-back and then a smooth mid-range pull-up jumper. Game Time! That wasn't luck. That was preparation meeting pressure.

But it doesn't stop there.

Fast forward to now. Those pressure-packed moments still come, just in different arenas. These days, I'm invited to speak live on industry podcasts and panels where there are no do overs, no cue cards, no second takes. It's just me, the host, and a whole production team pushing this episode out to hundreds, sometimes thousands of people across the world. Some of them are watching me for the first time, others have followed my work for years. Either way, the expectation is the same. Bring value, bring clarity and bring it now. The mic turns on, and it's go time. I understand the host's goals, I know the audience, and I trust that the work I've done and the wisdom I've earned will show up when it counts.

Then there's corporate life.

There was a moment in my career where I was tapped to present in front of senior executive leaders who had heard of me, who were familiar with the buzz around a talent acquisition best practice I'd championed internally, but this time, I had to show them. Not just talk about it in hallways or meetings, but actually demonstrate my expertise in a high-stakes boardroom setting. This wasn't just a casual conversation. This was strategy, data, process, and presentation all wrapped into one moment; and trust me, it was a test. A test of clarity. A test of confidence. A test of whether I could take what I knew and deliver it in a way that earned trust at the top. I walked in prepared, explained the methodology, backed it with results, answered every question without flinching. I watched the nods around the table multiply as I spoke. That day, not only did I pass the test, I thrived. Soon after, I was named process owner of the entire initiative.

What do all these moments have in common? I was ready when the moment found me. The tests will come in ways you expect and ways you don't. The goal isn't to avoid them. The goal is to thrive in them. And that only happens when your preparation is real and your belief in yourself is solid. Whether you're on the court, on a podcast, or in a boardroom, the lights will come on eventually. The question is, will you be ready to shine?

Whether it's an interview room, a boardroom, or your own side-hustle, the moment will come when someone asks you to turn potential into proof. That's the whole point of a skills assessment in interviewing. It's show and prove time. The interviewer wants to see you put your craft in motion, that's your edge. While other candidates scramble to remember talking points, you're ready to demonstrate what you got. Code that runs, data that speaks, designs that click, ideas that stick.

For many candidates, your opportunity to thrive in the hot seat during an interview will come in the form of that skills assessment. This is especially common in more technical roles like software engineering, data analysis, UX design where hiring managers want to see firsthand how well you code, solve, troubleshoot or build. Don't sleep on this if you're in a non-technical field either. In this digital age, even roles in operations, marketing or project management may require you to showcase digital fluency in real time. It may not always happen, but when it does, you need to be ready.

This reality was confirmed for me yet again when I was invited to a roundtable discussion with some of the top minds in the hiring space. What I discovered in that room only doubled down on the importance of sharpening your technical and digital skills and revealed just how high the bar is rising for candidates across every industry.

The Digital Skills Revolution

I vividly remember one Thursday afternoon, opening my inbox and seeing an email with the subject line: *"Exclusive Invitation: Roundtable Discussion in Chicago."* Instantly, I sat up a little straighter. My eyebrows raised, curiosity kicked in and I paused everything I was doing.

As I clicked in and began reading, it finally hit me. I had been handpicked. Not just noticed, but seen. The work I'd poured into the industry wasn't just making an impact. It was making a statement. This wasn't some generic blast email. This was personal. A well-respected organization was inviting me to the table, because they believed I had something real to contribute; and that hit differently.

I read it once, twice, three times, then smiled. Not out of arrogance, but out of gratitude, out of reflection. That moment reminded me of everything it had taken to get here. The long days, the coaching calls, the behind-the-scenes work. I thought about the candidates I coached, the DMs from job seekers, the career advice convos in random coffee shops. I knew this was bigger than me now. This wasn't just an invite, it was a responsibility. I was carrying all their stories with me into that room.

On the follow-up call with the event organizer, he shared exactly why I was chosen. As he spoke, I nodded quietly to myself. This is a mission. We wrapped the call, exchanged details for my flight and hotel and just like that, I was in full prep mode, selecting the right suit, shirt, tie combo and packing for that Chicago wind, because it's hit different.

On the flight to Chicago, I stared out the window, imagining the people who'd be around the table. What angles they might bring, what gaps I could fill, what truths I needed to say. Then the captain broke through the thoughts with an announcement: "Ladies and gentlemen, we are preparing for landing." As the plane started dipping through those thick Midwestern clouds, it began swaying side to side like it was trying to tell me something. I felt that breeze against the side of the plane and yeah, I knew right then why they call it the Windy City.

I touched down on a brisk spring afternoon and stepped into a gathering that felt like something out of a movie. An exclusive roundtable of tech leaders, workforce strategists, career coaches, recruiters, policy makers all seated together with one shared goal, to solve the growing challenges around tech talent, hiring and upskilling for minorities in a rapidly evolving workforce.

It felt like assembling with the Avengers, each of us with our own lane, our own specialty, our own superpower. But all united to talk strategy, impact and change. Just when the discussion was heating up, someone dropped a research stat on the table that shifted the whole energy in the room and doubled down on everything I had been sensing for months.

In February 2023, the National Skills Coalition joined forces with the Federal Reserve Bank of Atlanta's Center for Workforce & Economic Opportunity to release a report that hit us with a workforce wake-up call. Titled *Closing the Digital Skill Divide – The Payoff for Workers, Business, & The Economy*, this study didn't just scratch the surface, it dug deep into the digital demands of today's job market. What they uncovered was interesting, but not entirely surprising: 92% of job postings, even the ones labeled as "non-technical" still required either definitely digital or likely digital skills. We're not just talking tech roles. The research made it clear that this need is everywhere. From finance to manufacturing, every lane is being shaped by the digital era. Bookkeepers are now expected to be fluent in software like QuickBooks, and even manufacturing professionals are being asked to master AutoCAD, and other sophisticated design platform. This was a digital reality check for job seekers and employers alike.

Later that evening, after a long day of heavy discussion and even heavier notetaking, a few of us from the roundtable hit the town in true Chicago fashion. We found ourselves in a nice rooftop lounge, city lights dancing off the glass, suit jackets loosened and guards down. Over wings, a deep dish and a round of drinks, we kept the conversation going. The report from earlier that day kept coming up. It had all of us thinking and talking about what we were really seeing on the ground. Each person, from the career coach to the policy expert to the recruiting exec, echoed the same sentiment that the game is changing fast.

We shared real stories from our side of the hiring table; candidates who interviewed well but couldn't get through the technical phase. Others who soared because they came to play and put their real skills on display, showing up when it mattered most. One of the engineers in our crew leaned in and said, "Truth is, the skills assessment has become the lie detector in hiring. That moment stuck with me. We all nodded because we'd seen it ourselves. As the demand for technical and digital skills climbs, so does the expectation that candidates can back it up even more. More and more companies are leaning into assessments, especially in the tech scene. Not to intimidate candidates, but to make sure they're not just talking it, but actually walking it. That night reminded me that the hot seat isn't something to fear. It's a stage to show and prove.

How to Crack the Code to Thriving When Tested

After sitting through countless coaching sessions, resume reviews and webinars, one trend continues to surprise me. A lot of people still aren't clear on what actually qualifies as a skill. I know it might sound simple on the surface, but you'd be shocked how many people confuse exposure with expertise. Just dabbling in something or brushing up against it once doesn't mean you've mastered it. When you're being evaluated, especially in a skill-based assessment, that difference becomes very real.

Let's break it down. In my own words, a *true* skill is a learned ability that allows you to perform tasks, solve problems or deliver specific results. It comes from a mix of knowledge, hands-on practice and repeated refinement over time. A skill is something you can do, not just something you've seen done. It's something you can explain, demonstrate and confidently apply in real time, not just read about or copy once in a blue moon.

If you:

- Only did it briefly…
- Sat in on it but never tried it yourself…
- Learned it but never applied it…
- Wouldn't feel confident training someone on it…
- Threw it on your resume just to catch a recruiter's attention…

…it doesn't make the cut. At least, not as a skill that's ready for prime time.

That's why being real about your skills on your resume is so important, because if you list it, it's fair game for questioning. Interviewers can and will test it. It's all fair game, especially in fields like tech, where the stakes are high and precision matters.

One missed detail in a data pipeline, a rushed piece of bad code, or a weak infrastructure plan could cost a company real money or worse, open the door to a security breach. That's why technical skills get extra scrutiny.

From my time as a tech recruiter, I've seen this play out firsthand. I've watched interviewers analyze assessment results in debrief meetings, discussing strengths, gaps and what was missing. I've coached candidates before and after those assessments, some who nailed it, and others who got caught slipping.

A Technical Assessment is sometimes observed, but not always. Either way, the people reviewing it are usually subject matter experts, or even the hiring manager themselves. They're checking not just if you completed the task, but how you approached it, and whether you understood the trade-offs or decisions behind what you did. The best candidates show not just skill, but judgment.

Don't think this is just a "tech thing." It's not. Throughout my career, I've been on the job hunt myself even for roles in recruiting and leadership and I've had to complete assessments too. I've done everything from writing Boolean strings with minimal info, to building sample recruiting strategies off one-page case studies. I've done mock LinkedIn Recruiter searches and even drafted job descriptions with barely a sentence to go off. It's not about the industry it's about the level of trust a company wants in the hire they're about to make.

So, if you're preparing for a skills assessment or might be facing one soon, understand that assessments are truth-tellers. They separate the surface-level from the skilled. Up next, I'll break down what you need to know to walk into a skills assessment with clarity and confidence and actually thrive in that hot seat. Let's get into it.

Understand the Assessment Format

Before you go into any assessment, know what you're walking into. For tech professionals, this might look like a coding challenge, system design simulation, or debugging task. For non-tech roles, it could be a business case, a writing prompt or a problem-solving exercise using structured thinking. Make sure you understand what platform the assessment is being delivered on and what tools are fair game. For tech assessments, that might mean access to a virtual whiteboard or notes. Also clarify how much time you have, whether it's timed, live with someone watching or a take home project. The format and setup will tell you a lot about how to prepare.

Know the Core Skill Being Tested

Every assessment is built around a specific skill or competency. In tech, that might be front-end vs. back-end development, systems design, cloud engineering or data structures. In engineering, it could be SolidWorks, AutoCAD or reading schematics. In accounting or finance, Excel or Power BI might be it. For non-tech roles, you might be tested on your ability to analyze data, write clearly, build a plan or use industry tools. Don't assume. It's better to ask and prepare accordingly.

Brush Up Through Practice

If it's been a minute since you've done a certain task, now's the time to sharpen up. Get with a coach, a mentor or someone you trust who's deep in the field. Ask them what they've seen on assessments and how they'd approach it. Use bootcamps, practice sites or free online resources to sharpen your skills. If mock tests are available, take them! Aim to reach at least a medium proficiency level and then challenge yourself to keep climbing. Start at beginner level if you need to, but don't stop there.

Simulate the Real Thing

If you're serious about passing the test, don't just wing it. Simulate the full experience. Take your mock test on the same laptop you'll use, at the same time of day, in the same setting. Set a timer, close your tabs and focus. Think of it like game-day prep or a dress rehearsal. The more familiar you are with the setup, the less likely you'll be thrown off when the lights are on.

Be Ready to Talk Through It

Don't assume the work speaks for itself. You need to speak for it too. Interviewers want to know your thinking. What did you prioritize? Why that solution? Were there other ways you could've approached it? What were the trade-offs? This shows maturity in your thinking and depth in your skills. If you don't know something, don't fake it. Walk them through how you'd figure it out. That's just as valuable.

Thriving when tested isn't just about talent. It's about preparation, mindset and composure under pressure. Whether it's an interview, a live assessment or a game-changing moment at work, there will come a time when you have to show and prove. Your resume might get you in the door. Your story might spark interest, but what seals the deal is your ability to execute when it counts.

In today's job market, digital fluency and technical readiness are the standard, not the bonus. Employers aren't just looking for potential; they want proof. So, study the playbook. Rehearse your game plan. Put yourself in real situations before the real moment comes. The hot seat is inevitable, but when you've done the work, it's not pressure, it's your platform.

Don't just survive it. Sit in it like you belong there. Because you do.

Chapter 8

Networking Is a Value Exchange
Give Game, Get Growth

Reason #8: Not Leveraging Your Network Effectively

When most people think about getting a job or leveling up in their career, the first things that come to mind are resumes and interviews. That's where all the hype is. Those are the plays everyone's rehearsing, but there's another move. One that's not always front and center but stays clutch when it counts. And that's Networking.

Just the word "networking" alone can make some people tighten up. For a lot of us, it feels awkward, forced, or even intimidating. You walk into a room full of people in shiny shoes and stiff collars, and your brain's already racing: "What do I say? Am I doing this right? Do I belong here?" Trust me, that feeling is more common than people let on.

Here's the thing, networking isn't just about small talk and business cards. At its core, it's about connection. It's about finding common ground, building real relationships and exchanging game. Yes, real game. Whether that's career advice, job leads, life lessons or just a gem that shifts your mindset, networking is a two-way street. You give something of value, and in return, you get growth. It's iron sharpening iron, in real time.

It doesn't always have to happen in a ballroom or a Zoom meeting either. Sometimes the best networking moments happen in the most unexpected places, a cookout, a group chat or even a random run-in at the coffee shop. Some of the most powerful career moves start with a simple, genuine conversation rooted in shared experiences, mutual respect and curiosity.

This chapter is about shifting the mindset on how we see networking. Not as something to dread or avoid, but as a tool that can unlock opportunities, expand your reach and connect you to the people who will challenge you, vouch for you and grow with you. It's time to stop seeing networking as a chore and start seeing it for what it really is, a value exchange. Let's get into it.

The Digital Dash: Your LinkedIn Better Keep Up

LinkedIn changed the game, and the rules forever. What once took months of networking events, awkward coffee meetups and phone tag now happens with a few clicks and a solid profile. In today's digital era, LinkedIn is the front-runner, the undefeated champion of professional social networking platforms. It's not just a place to "be seen" it's where real connections, collaborations and career-changing moments are made. With hundreds of millions of users, it has planted its flag as the go-to destination for hiring teams, recruiters and job seekers around the world. The fact is, if you're on the job market and your LinkedIn profile is weak or nonexistent? You might be missing opportunities you don't even know about.

Over the course of my recruiting career, I've spent a lot of time on LinkedIn, more than most. From tech to engineering, life sciences to marketing, I've sat alongside hiring managers in LinkedIn souring sessions. That's when, for 30 minutes or so, the hiring manager and I team up like co-pilots and comb through profiles together, trying to find that one right candidate to bring in for an interview. These sessions move fast, like a digital dash across the site. You've got specific search terms, tight goals and a small window of time. Just like we do with resumes, we analyze LinkedIn profiles for alignment with the role. What still shocks me is how many job seekers don't treat their LinkedIn with the same care as their resume.

Some profiles are just blank slates, no "About" section, no skills listed, no visible work history or impact. That's not just a missed opportunity; it's a red flag. Because in the eyes of a recruiter or hiring manager, an empty profile doesn't inspire confidence. It pushes us to move on, fast and keep searching for someone who shows they care about how they show up online. Your LinkedIn isn't just a digital resume, it's your brand billboard, your 24/7 digital hype reel, your career's front door. If your resume says, "here's what I've done," your LinkedIn should say, "here's how I do it, why I love it and what I'm ready to do next." In short, your resume shows your game, but your LinkedIn? That's sets the frame.

Now let's talk sourcing, because that's the behind-the-scenes magic most people don't know about. In supply chain and ops, "sourcing" means finding the right vendors to supply what a company needs to function. In recruiting, it means identifying and locating the right people with the right skills at the right time. That's where tools like LinkedIn Recruiter come in. These are special tools built into LinkedIn just for employers, giving us access to filters, tags, past interactions and profile insights that regular users don't see. When we're sourcing candidates, we're not just looking at whether your title matches, we're looking for the full package: content, consistency, skills, experience and impact.

So, in today's landscape, having a polished LinkedIn profile isn't optional. It's part of your professional playbook. If your profile isn't telling your story, it might be telling nothing at all. Don't let an incomplete digital presence be the reason you get passed over. The same way your resume deserves effort and attention, so does your LinkedIn. Think of it as your career co-pilot in this digital first world. The next opportunity might be one recruiter search away.

Let me let you in on something most people don't know. Your LinkedIn profile gets viewed more than you think, and most of the time, before your resume. I've sat side by side with hiring managers, scrolling through LinkedIn profiles with a tight deadline and a head full of business needs.

Here's what we really see:

We see the blank or unprofessional headshot and wonder if this is a real person.

We see a missing headline and ask ourselves, *"Do they even know what they want?"*

We see an empty experience section and think, *"They can't be serious."*

We click off in seconds, not because you aren't talented, but because your LinkedIn said nothing to make us believe otherwise.

On the flip side, when your page is right? When it reflects your wins, your growth, your skillset and your energy? We pause. We lean in. We read. Just like a resume.

It's not about being flashy. It's about being smart. A solid photo that actually looks like you. A banner image that sets the tone. A headline that tells me what you're passionate about. Experience that shows what you've done. Keywords that help us find you. A link to your portfolio that shows you've been doing the work, even if nobody handed you the title yet.

You don't have to be famous, but you do have to show up like you're ready to be seen. So, the next time you wonder why no one's reaching out, ask yourself, "If I landed on my own profile, would I stop and be curious or would I keep scrolling?"

Let's say your profile is polished, tight and looking like it belongs. Your headshot clean, your headline solid, your experience reads like a highlight reel. Now what?

What do you do with that great profile? Because even the most fire profile won't work for you if you're not putting it in motion. That's when the real game starts, making your presence felt in a way that's intentional, strategic and meaningful.

First of all, please bypass the small talk. This is not the time for "Hey" or "Hope you're well" messages with no direction or substance. In the world of recruiting, especially during heavy hiring seasons or when roles are moving fast, every message is a moment. Recruiters, especially the good ones are juggling interviews, offer negotiations, hiring manager syncs and sourcing sprints. Trust me, I've been that recruiter running on coffee and calendar invites. When a DM comes through, it needs to hit with purpose. Say who you are, what you're about and what you're looking for, clearly and respectfully.

Don't go overboard. I've opened messages that felt like somebody copied and pasted their whole autobiography with plot twists, life updates and a dozen questions at once. Listen, I respect the hustle, but nobody's reading nine paragraphs in between Zoom calls. A great message is like a solid elevator pitch. Short, personal and clear on what you want. That's how you break through the noise.

Before you even send that DM, you should've already been active. The secret sauce isn't just in messaging someone. It's in being visible before you need something. Connect with intention. Like their posts. Leave a thoughtful comment. Follow the people who are consistently giving game; those recruiters, hiring managers and leaders who drop gems, share real jobs or spark discussions in your industry. We all notice who shows up in our notifications. So, when your message finally hits, your name already rings a bell. That familiarity changes everything. You go from "just another message" to "wait, I know them, they've been showing love."

That's the real cheat code: visibility plus value equals opportunity.

Sometimes You Gotta Play the Long Game

By now, you understand how powerful LinkedIn networking can be especially when done right. Platforms like LinkedIn have made it easier than ever to make meaningful professional connections with just a few clicks. As game changing as online networking is, we can't forget about the power of being in the room.

There's something different, something real about face-to-face interactions. The energy. The body language. The vibe. That unspoken connection you pick up on when you're not just behind a screen but standing across from someone, sharing a laugh, dropping game or exchanging insight. That's the kind of interaction that sticks with people.

And what better way to show you than with a story. Let's talk about something that stops a lot of people from tapping into the true potential of networking, and that's impatience.

We live in a fast-paced world where we expect quick results. Networking, especially the in-person kind, often works on a different timeline. It's not always about instant payoff. It's about planting seeds. Building rapport. Showing up consistently and authentically, even when there's no guarantee of immediate return, because when those seeds grow, they can lead to real opportunities, real relationships and real career growth for everyone involved.

So now, let me take you into a moment from my own life that captures exactly what it looks like to stay ready, play the long game and see the rewards of genuine in-person connection unfold.

The year was 2022, and North Carolina was already heating up like it had something to prove. Summer had officially clocked in; my favorite season hands down. There's just something about the longer days, the smell of barbeque in the air and the freedom to move how you want that always hit different. I was outside and intentional, ready to soak up the sunshine and opportunities alike. On this particular summer, networking was at the top of my agenda.

Now, if you know anything about the tech industry, you know summer through Thanksgiving is what we call conference season, and I mean prime time. It's like the All-Star circuit for tech. Every corner of the industry pulls up: job seekers, recruiters, hiring managers, innovators, dreamers, builders; you name it. The energy is unmatched. Picture rooms buzzing with activity; insightful panels, skill-packed workshops, real-time interviews, keynote mic drops and of course, the late-night after-parties backed by corporate sponsors trying to make their presence felt. These weren't just events, they were entire ecosystems of possibility.

By then, I was about six months into my role as a Senior Lead Tech Recruiter at one of the largest and most recognized tech companies on the planet. I wasn't just attending; I had a mission. I was on the hunt for top-tier diverse tech talent, and I knew exactly where to look. That journey led me to none other than Atlanta, GA; a city that, in the tech world, was coming up strong and fast. With Silicon Valley giants setting up shop in the heart of the South, Atlanta wasn't just a tech hub anymore. It was the destination, and when it came to Black tech excellence, Atlanta stood tall.

Dubbed "Black Hollywood," ATL has it all, political power, economic pull and a deep, undeniable cultural influence. The same place where hip-hop legends built empires and black filmmakers told our stories was now becoming a 'launch-pad' for Black professionals in tech. For someone like me, it wasn't just inspiring, it was a call to action.

I packed with purpose. I gathered my sharpest conference fits, a suitcase full of branded company swag, and a mindset ready to build real connections. Once I arrived at Raleigh-Durham International Airport, I was all systems go. Even though Atlanta was a familiar city for me, the anticipation never wore off. As my plane touched down at Hartsfield-Jackson, I followed tradition, quick texts to my mom and big sister. Just a simple, "Landed safe.

Love y'all." Those small check-ins always meant everything to them. After all, keeping worry at bay was a priority.

Exiting the plane, I was greeted by the pulse of Atlanta. Warm air, big energy and a sense that something special was already brewing. I was in my typical travel uniform: my go-to black Adidas tracksuit, Yeezy Boost 350s keeping me comfortable yet stylish, and of course, my signature all-black Versace shades resting on my face like armor. These weren't just travel clothes, they were part of my ritual. Wherever I flew, this look helped me feel grounded, confident and unmistakably myself.

As I made my way through Hartsfield-Jackson, weaving between terminals and escalators, I caught the attention of a couple of ladies going the opposite direction. One had the long, flowing knotless braids that cascaded down her back. The other rocked the natural, wavy hair that bounced freely with her movement. They gave me that look. You know, that warm, playful but curious look; subtle but definitely not mistaken. Peeking through my black Versace shades, I gave a respectful nod paired with a smooth smirk. One of them smiled back and said playfully, "Hey, King." I grinned just a bit, but in my head, I was like, *Okay ATL, I see you already.*

I hadn't even hit the city yet and I was already being embraced.

With my bag now in hand and my feet officially on Georgia soil, I exchanged quick hellos with some coworkers who had also flown in for the event, but there was no time to waste. This conference was one of the ones. A premiere tech experience rooted in Atlanta. This annual gathering brought out everybody; software engineers, startup founders, tech recruiters, industry leaders, all under one roof. It wasn't just about tech; it was about culture, connection and belonging.

The next morning, we set up at our booth, armed with company swag and conversation. As waves of attendees floated by, each interaction started blending into the next until one stood out.

John.

He approached with purpose, his energy sharp and it wasn't long before we found our common ground; a shared dedication to nonprofit work advancing people of color in tech. That shifted the whole conversation. He wasn't just checking boxes; this man had vision. As we peeled back the layers, I learned John was a seasoned engineer at a well-known tech company, but even more impressive, he was also the founder of his own tech consulting business that was gaining serious traction. I was impressed, but more than that, I was inspired.

In the middle of the conference chaos, John casually mentioned he was planning an event of his own in Atlanta and was looking for sponsors. I saw the opportunity. I told him, "Say less," and made a mental note to track down my coworker who handles all things sponsorships for the company. I let John know we'd be hosting a company takeover that night at one of the restaurants in Ponce City Market. I told him to pull up. I'd introduce him directly to the decision-maker. We dapped up, exchanged info and he disappeared back into the crowd. I had a feeling that this connection was one of those that was going to mean something later.

Back at the hotel, I decided to unwind and catch up on some ESPN, only to be reminded that Game 1 of the NBA Finals was happening the same night as our company's after-party event. That little sports fan dilemma kicked in, do I show up or stay and watch the game? Duty called, and so did opportunity. After a quick shower and change into something fresh, I ordered an Uber and made my way to Ponce City Market.

The venue was immaculately decorated. Soft lighting, bold signage, the energy in the room already dialed up to ten. It was filled with tech professionals, creatives and corporate sponsors, all eager to connect and have a good time. You could feel the hum of conversations and opportunity mixing in the air like a good playlist.

As the night unfolded, I found myself moving through the room, talking shop with job seekers and potential collaborators, sharing insight into open roles with the tech giant I proudly represented. Between conversations, I glanced at my phone for Finals updates; old habits die hard.

Then, through the dimmed lights and curated crowd, a familiar face emerged, it was John. We dapped up like old friends, instantly picking up where we left off earlier in the day. We swapped stories from our conversations with attendees, each of us impressed by the talent in the room. I made good on my promise, tracking down my co-worker who handled corporate sponsorships. Once I found her, I didn't waste time. I introduced the two, gave them a quick backstory and stepped aside to let the magic happen.

Later on, John circled back with a grin on his face that said it all. "I got her contact info," he told me. "We're setting up a follow-up meeting next week." A networking win.

As the event wound down and people began to trickle out into the Atlanta night, I took a moment to take it all in; the conversations, the connections, the possibilities. Then I dipped out and headed back to the hotel.

The next day, I boarded my flight back to Raleigh, NC, not just with cool memories and a few extra company T-shirts in my suitcase, but with something far more valuable and that was new relationships that would pay dividends down the line.

But the story doesn't end there…

As autumn rolled in, John and I reconnected later that year for a follow-up conversation. This time, the setting was more relaxed just two professionals chopping it up, catching up on life and goals. John had a simple ask; he wanted my eyes on his resume. He trusted my insight, and I was happy to offer my perspective, but as we dug into his resume, the conversation took an unexpected turn.

That's when I found out John wasn't just a talented engineer and entrepreneur. He was also the host of a respected podcast in the tech space. And just like that, he hit me with an invite. He thought the advice I'd just dropped on him about resumes and career storytelling could benefit his audience too. No pitch deck, no long back and forth. Just genuine respect and an opportunity to build.

Without hesitation, I said yes. When we recorded that episode, I didn't hold back. I showed up, spoke my truth and gave his listeners the same game I've always given to the people I've mentored. That appearance opened the floodgates. Before I knew it, I was being invited to speak on other industry podcasts, adding value to new audiences and stepping fully into my voice as not just a recruiter, but a thought leader.

Fast forward to the rainy days of Spring 2023. An invitation arrived in my inbox that made me sit back, smile wide and just say, *"Wow."* I had been asked to be a guest on the most prominent Black tech podcast in the game. The excitement? Unmatched. The honor? Deep. As someone who had been a loyal supporter of this platform and respected the brilliance of its host, the moment meant everything. This wasn't just a podcast. It was "the podcast." A space reserved for the Who's Who of tech. Landing a spot here meant something. It meant that your name held weight, that your work spoke volumes and that your voice was going to be magnified to brand new levels. If you did well on this pod, you were on your way to superstardom in the industry.

So, another trip to Atlanta was on the books, but this time, it wasn't for the glitz of a tech conference. It was to record an episode that I knew had the potential to shift the trajectory of my career. With now well over 1 million subscribers, a massive Instagram following, and episodes that racked up tens of thousands of views, the platform's reach was undeniable. And now, my voice, my story was about to be part of it.

On that solo trip down, I flipped through my contacts, reaching out to friends and industry peers in the city. One of the first people

I hit up was John. We linked up the day before my recording and grabbed a meal. Our conversation? It was like an unreleased podcast episode of its own. We were talking through tech news, industry trends and the growing demand for digital skills. As we wrapped up, John leaned in and asked, "So what brings you to the city this time?" That's when I let him in on the news. "I'm a guest, recording live on a podcast tomorrow." He said, "Oh yeah, which one?" I told him the name of the pod and the host. His face lit up with pure excitement. He gave me my flowers right there on the spot, congratulating me and reminding me how big that platform really was. Before we parted ways, he told me, "You should definitely drop some of what we talked about in that episode." I nodded and his encouragement stuck with me.

The next morning, I stepped into the studio and recorded what would soon become one of the most-viewed episodes for the next several months. Thousands of views poured in, LinkedIn messages started filling my inbox, and the Instagram follower count skyrocketed, but the story didn't end there.

Later that year, I was filling a tech role based in – `````you guessed it, Atlanta; and guess who came to mind immediately? John. I reached out, and the fit was perfect. After a few interviews, he landed the offer. The very same guy who once stopped by my booth at a tech conference just to introduce himself now had a new role, thanks in part to the relationship we built from that moment on.

That first handshake turned into an introduction to a sponsor...which turned into a resume review…which turned into a podcast invitation…which turned into a moment of encouragement…which turned into a successful hire. Full circle. That's the power of true networking. When it's built on shared values and mutual respect, it turns into something real. It creates moments where both people walk away better than they were before. That's not just networking; it's value exchange in its highest form.

How to Crack the Code to Effective Networking

If there's one truth about networking that often gets lost in translation, it's this; the best networks are built on reciprocity. That simple exchange of value what you bring versus what you take is the lifeline of meaningful connection. But too often, people fumble the ball. They approach networking like it's a solo mission, laser-focused on what they need: a job, a connect, an opportunity. Don't get it twisted, there's nothing wrong with wanting something. But if your only move is to ask, you're playing short-term ball in a long-term game.

Networking is community work, and real communities are built on contribution. Instead of pulling up to every conversation wondering, "What can they do for me?", try flipping it to "What can I offer?" It could be your insight, your connections, your encouragement or even just your time. That kind of mindset shift is how you become unforgettable. And the best part? When your time comes, and it will, you'll be surrounded by people ready to pour back into you.

Take John's story. When we met, he didn't hit me with a pitch or a resume immediately. He led with purpose, his work in the nonprofit tech space, his passion for education and his vision for bridging the digital divide. That initial connection turned into an opportunity, a podcast feature and eventually a job for him. Why? Because value was exchanged at every stage.

Deposits & Withdrawals

Think of networking like a bank account. Every connection you make is an account you open. Every time you support, uplift or share something of value, you're making a deposit, but if all you ever do is ask for favors, recommendations or hookups without ever contributing, you're making constant withdrawals. Eventually, you'll overdraft on that relationship.

You want your relationships to feel mutually fulfilling, not transactional. Be someone who adds value to a room, not someone who always drains the energy from it. People can feel the difference between authenticity and desperation. And trust, value always gets noticed.

Make It Last Forever

Real connections don't die after the conference badge comes off. They grow roots when you take the time to find common ground that has nothing to do with titles or resumes. During my conversation with John, we didn't just talk shop, we talked culture, purpose and shared values. That's what made it stick.

Networking isn't about being memorable for your elevator pitch. It's about being memorable for your presence. When you take a genuine interest in people for who they are, what they care about, where they come from; you become the kind of person people want in their corner. As Dale Carnegie said: "You can make more friends in two months by becoming interested in others than you can in two years by trying to get them interested in you." And he was right.

Know What You Carry

One of the coolest parts of networking is discovering your own value. Everybody's carrying something. Maybe you've got deep industry knowledge. Maybe you're good at making people feel seen. Maybe you're the plug for resume help, or you're the one who always knows about new tech trends. Whatever it is, own it.

John had five things working in his favor: his engineering knowledge, his own company, a podcast platform, insight into Atlanta's tech scene and a coaching lens. There will be people in the room who will care about at least one of those things. That's powerful. When you walk into a room, know that you're not empty handed. Your experiences, skills, and energy are currency. Use them well.

Not Every Connection Is Meant to Be

Not every connection is meant to be your next breakthrough. And that's okay. Some people won't respond, won't follow up or just won't vibe with your energy. That's not a reflection of your worth, it's redirection toward the people and spaces that are actually aligned. The real ones? They'll find you. Stay authentic and keep showing up.

There Are Hidden Gems in Unexpected Places

Volunteering is one of the most slept-on networking strategies in the game. Some of the most powerful, well-connected people are also the most generous with their time. I've seen executives in company-branded hoodies bagging lunches at community events or mentoring at youth hackathons. That's your opening. Not a cold email. Not a random DM. A moment of shared purpose.

Don't Go at It Alone

For my introverts; Yes, you can win at networking too. You don't have to fake being the loudest person in the room. Bring a friend, wingman or even a mentor to your next event. Sometimes all it takes is a familiar face to help you find your rhythm. Confidence doesn't always show up loud. Sometimes it's quiet, steady and exactly what the room needs.

Looking for a job isn't just about a strong resume or sharp interview answers. It's about having the right people in your corner. Think of your favorite action movie. Just when the hero's about to lose, their squad shows up and shifts the momentum. That's what your network does. These MVPs rally behind you, boost your confidence and help you push through when the hustle gets heavy.

At the center of that squad? Enter **The Sensei aka *The Coach*.** Even the greatest need guidance. Serena had a coach; so did MJ, Tiger and Brady. The best don't go it alone. A great coach doesn't just hype you up, they prepare you. They give you strategy, sharpen your skills and speak the truth, even when it stings. Their feedback may not always feel good, but it hits different when it helps you bounce back sharper than ever.

As you build your network, keep an eye out for these key players like The Sensei who can help you get ahead. They're out there, and we'll break down a few more MVPs you'll want to have on your team and in your network.

Meet **The Trailblazer, aka "The Mentor"**, your guiding light in the job search hustle. This is someone you admire, who's already navigated the road you're on and can offer wisdom from the other side. Likely from your target industry, they're not always available, but when they speak, it hits every time.

Think of that iconic 1997 NBA moment. A young Kobe Bryant asking Michael Jordan mid-game how to master the fadeaway. MJ dropped a quick gem, and Kobe turned it into one of the most legendary moves in his own arsenal. That's what mentors do; one insight can shift your whole game.

So be intentional. Don't waste the moment. Set clear expectations, come prepared, ask good questions and apply what you learn. Make your mentor proud. Your Trailblazer might already be in your network. Pay attention and reach out.

Welcome **The Godfather (or The Godmother), aka "The Sponsor."** This isn't your everyday advocate. We're talking about someone with major pull. A sponsor is a respected heavyweight whose influence can open doors most people didn't even know existed. When they speak, the room listens. When they co-sign, people move.

The truth is, you don't just get a sponsor, you earn one. It's like receiving a high-level stamp of approval. They'll likely watch you from afar first, making sure you're solid, consistent and worth the social capital they're putting on the line. It's not shade; it's strategy.

When you do gain their trust, though? It's a game-changer. Opportunities, invites and conversations you once dreamed about suddenly become reachable. So, if you've got a Godfather or Godmother in your circle, nurture that bond. If you don't yet; stay ready, stay visible and keep putting in the work. They might already be watching.

Introducing **The Lobbyist aka "The Advocate."** In the fast-paced world of job hunting, this is your personal hype team. The best part? You can have more than one. In fact, you should. Advocates are those peers in your network who vouch for your character, integrity and work ethic when you're not in the room. They may not be the final decision-makers, but their proximity to influence makes their voice matter.

Think of them as your behind-the-scenes promo crew. These could be co-workers, collaborators or industry peers who've seen you in action and speak highly of your professionalism from a front-row seat. Don't sleep on them.

It's easy to chase mentors, coaches and sponsors and you should, but your advocates are often the bridge to those higher-level connections. In my own job-seeking journey, it was often the quiet push from an advocate that got me into doors I didn't even know were open. They shared my name, gave a good word and created opportunity all because we had built real respect through everyday work and real conversation. Never underestimate the power of your peers.

Meet **The Multiplier aka "The Connector."** We all know that person. The social glue in every circle, the one who's on a first-name basis with everybody. Think of them as the walking LinkedIn algorithm. Whether they've been crowned a "Top LinkedIn Voice" or just have a phone full of decision-makers and dream-job plugs, they've built a network that actually works. Their digital presence is active, their real-life Rolodex is elite and a quick call or intro from them holds weight.

The Connector doesn't just know people, they multiply opportunities. They can shift your whole career trajectory with a single introduction, an email thread or a well-placed name drop at the right time. They see how people and purpose align and are generous with the connections they believe in. They may not always have the job for you, but they likely know someone who does.

And that's the point: your MVPs don't all play the same role, but The Connector makes sure the right people are in the room when your name comes up. They're not just part of your circle. They expand it.

Networking isn't just about collecting business cards or growing your follower count. It's about building a community of real people who help each other rise. When done right, it's a value exchange that creates momentum, connections that spark confidence, introductions that change lives and conversations that lead to rooms you never imagined being in. As we've seen through the stories and insights in this chapter, the people you meet along the way, the Coaches, Mentors, Sponsors, Advocates and Connectors aren't just titles. They're the real MVPs who can help shift the networking game for you.

Remember, you're not just a receiver in this process, you're a playmaker too. You carry something valuable: your story, your skill set, your perspective. Don't downplay it. Show up, offer game and stay open to growth. The most impactful networking happens when we give as much as we hope to gain.

Whether on LinkedIn or in person, whether it's a conference in Atlanta or a volunteer event in your own city, show up, be real and stay ready. The relationships you build today might just be the reason your name gets mentioned in the right room tomorrow.

So, the next time you hesitate to reach out or walk up to someone new, remember, one genuine connection can change your career. Give game. Get growth, and never forget, the network you build might just be the bridge to everything you've been working toward.

Chapter 9

Invisible Filters
The Bias You Don't See,
But Definitely Feel

Reason #9: Bias in Hiring

There's this one interview I had early in my career that I still think about sometimes. This time, I was the candidate. It wasn't for a flashy job with a six-figure salary or a big, impressive title. On paper, it was the right move to gain some real experience, but what happened in that room never left me. To this very day, I remember exactly how it made me feel.

Many years ago, I was trying to take the next step in my recruiting career, looking to move beyond junior-level duties into something with more ownership. More weight. More impact. I was hungry to move beyond entry-level work, to finally get a seat at the table. I'd been putting in the work, learning the ropes, sharpening my recruiting skills, stacking my small wins. I didn't have the name recognition yet though, but I was on the way. This was well before anyone knew my name, before the speaking gigs, the awards and LinkedIn recognition, before I walked into rooms and saw faces light up.

I prepared for that interview like a pro. I showed up early, wore a nicely tailored suit I'd stretched my budget to afford, got a fresh haircut and brought a few crisp copies of my resume in hand. I was locked in, ready to walk in there and prove I was the right guy for the job.

However, the moment I stepped into the room, I felt it. You ever walk into a space and feel something shift? The energy dipped. The air got a little heavier. The handshake I received was limp and cold. The eye contact was shifty. Something was off, and for a brief second, I started to question myself. Did I miss something?

Doubts crept in, but I knew better. I had checked myself in the mirror before I walked in. Tie straight, shoulders back, confidence on point, but whatever image they were expecting when they read my name and saw my resume... let's just say it wasn't me.

They kept calling me "young man," but not in the warm, respectful tone your auntie might use. This was different. Condescending. Cold. Dismissive. Like a reminder that I wasn't one of them. They asked me what I liked to do outside of work. I gave a genuine answer, something real about who I was. The interviewer chuckled and said, "Yeah, figured you'd say that. We're not really into those kinds of things here." I sat with that for a second.

Then came the question: "Where are you from originally?" The way he asked it wasn't just curiosity. It was like he was trying to solve a mystery, like I didn't quite belong, as if I was on the wrong part of town and he was trying to figure out why.

I asked why that mattered. He said something about "culture fit" and wanting to make sure the team would feel comfortable with whoever they brought in. Funny, none of those things aligned with the "values" displayed on the company's webpage.

They barely asked me anything about the actual role. Two questions, max, that had anything to do with my skills or experience. The rest was a performance. The lead interviewer couldn't even look me in the eyes.

Still, I showed up. I answered everything clearly and confidently, because I knew I was qualified. I knew I had the experience. I knew I did everything right, but deep down, I also knew the decision had already been made. I wasn't being assessed for what I could do. I was being dismissed for who I was.

Not even an hour later, I was back in my car, headed to my small one-bedroom apartment when the rejection email hit my inbox. No personal message. No phone call. Just An auto-response.

They never saw me. Not really. They only saw what they assumed, and that's the part that stung, because I knew I'd done everything right.

That's what bias often feels like. It's not always loud. It doesn't always come with slurs or clear violations. Sometimes, it's quiet. Dismissive. Distant. It hides behind smiles, coded language and "gut feelings." You don't always see it, but you feel it; and when it shows up in a room you've worked so hard to get into, it cuts deep, because it tells you that no matter how qualified, polished or prepared you are, some people only ever see your difference.

From that day forward, everything I did in my career carried a different kind of weight. A different kind of fire. Whether I was pushing hiring teams to expand their candidate slates to include more diverse talent, making sure a candidates had the right accommodations to shine or spending my evenings volunteering at HBCUs to prep students for their first interviews. There was a deeper purpose behind every move I made.

I wasn't just recruiting talent anymore. I was building bridges. I was keeping the door open behind me. I was making sure someone else got a fair shot, whether it was someone who looked like me or someone who didn't. People who came from where I came from, or those who didn't. It was for those who maybe never had the luxury of being seen past the surface.

That journey didn't just land me job titles. It led me to leadership. I was called to serve, stepping into Presidential roles for two of the largest Black professional non-profit organizations in the world. One focused on increasing representation of black professionals in tech, the other, dedicated to elevating Black excellence across the business world and beyond. It wasn't luck. It wasn't a fluke. It was purpose. It was destiny.

In this chapter, we're not sugarcoating anything.

We're going to call things exactly what they are. We're going to break down the many faces of bias that show up, from the ones you can spot from a mile away to the ones that creep in quietly. Some of these filters are built into systems, others are built into people. Either way, you need to know what you're up against, not so you second guess your worth, but so you never forget it.

You're not imagining it. It's not just in your head. Once we name it, we can talk about how to move through it, around it and sometimes, how to avoid it altogether.

Because your success isn't about changing who you are. It's about understanding the game, then choosing your strategy accordingly.

Hiring by Vibe: How Bias Blocks Talent

Let's just keep it real! We all have biases. It lives in all of us in some way, whether we're ready to admit it or not. That includes me. That includes you, and that includes the most well-intentioned person you know. Bias doesn't automatically make you a bad person. It doesn't mean you're out to harm people or intentionally discriminate, but what it does mean is that you've probably been shaped by your upbringing, your environment, your culture or your experiences. Sometimes, without even realizing it, those things influence how we see others. How we judge their "fit."

How we define "qualified." It can also define who we choose to believe in.

Now, don't get me wrong, there are some people out there who are up to no good, but it's my genuine belief that most people I've met in this industry mean well. Good intentions don't always protect us or the people we're evaluating from the harm bias can cause. That's why we have to stay aware, as opposed to pointing the finger towards others, but checking ourselves too.

There are all kinds of biases that show up. I won't pretend I've seen them all, but I've experienced enough of them, sometimes as a recruiter watching it play out, and sometimes as a candidate on the receiving end. Here are a few biases I've seen up close. There are many others, but these are the ones I know most about, have hit the hardest and that stuck with me the most.

Affinity Bias

This happens when we favor people who feel familiar to us. People who went to the same school, grew up in the same kind of neighborhood, root for the same team or share the same hobbies. Listen, there's absolutely nothing wrong with finding common ground with people; actually, it's encouraged. That's part of being human, but it becomes an issue when that's the only ground we stand on. When decisions start leaning more toward "who we vibe with" instead of "who's the most capable," we've already missed the mark.

Confirmation Bias

This one's a little trick. It creeps in when we walk into interviews already carrying a belief or assumption about someone and then spend the entire conversation looking for evidence to prove ourselves right. Maybe we think the candidate isn't a strong communicator, so every pause suddenly feels like a red flag. Perhaps we assume they're too laid back or introverted and ignore how thoughtful, strategic or high achieving they actually are. It's like building a case against someone without letting the full story unfold.

Gender Bias

This one is simple. It's the quick judgment we may make about someone because of their gender. Sometimes the bias shows up in deeply rooted societal expectations. We can make assumptions about their leadership style, personality or priorities. I've seen people penalized for being "too assertive" or "not assertive enough," and the root of that criticism was directly linked more to gender than merit.

Halo/Horns Effect

This one hits in two different ways. The halo effect is when you see one specific thing about a candidate that is great, and you let that drive the entire evaluation. Rather than accessing the candidate entirely, you latch on to one thing and one thing only as the end all be all. The horns effect hits the opposite. This is when you latch onto one "perceived" negative and can't let it go, instead of viewing things from a larger viewpoint. Either way, you're making a whole decision based on the tiniest piece of information. An example of this is declaring that a candidate is "destined for greatness" or "doomed for failure" only because they worked at a big-name company. I know from first-hand experience that this is not always the case.

Racial Bias

This one cuts the deepest. Racial bias is layered, historic and deeply rooted. Racial bias can show up often in quiet, but powerful ways. It happens when someone's race, culture or background becomes the lens through which someone's entire candidacy is viewed. Instead of being judged on their skills or experience, they're evaluated based on stereotypes and assumptions. Of all the biases, this one tends to be the most harmful, not just professionally, but personally as well.

So then comes the question, if people can't manage their biases, why not remove them from the equation? If bias is the problem, maybe technology is the solution. That was the idea.

Let algorithms take over. Faster. Fairer. Smarter. Remove the emotion, focus on the data, and make hiring about qualifications, nothing more. On the surface, it felt like progress, but beneath it, new questions started to rise. Could technology actually make the process perfect? How exactly will an algorithm eliminate bias? Can technology really provide a fair and equitable assessment?

Something extremely powerful has now arrived, and it has shifted the culture.

However, we still have questions. We're still searching for something deeper.

We still want The Answer.

The Crossover We Didn't See Coming

Let's talk about AI, and no, not artificial intelligence, well at least not just yet. I'm talking about the AI who wore cornrows, rocked tattoos, wore oversized jerseys and left defenders frozen with that iconic crossover. For a long time, especially in the Black community, he was the only "AI" we acknowledged. A Hall of Famer from Hampton, Virginia, Allen Iverson was more than just a basketball player, he was a cultural shift. He was a movement. He earned the nickname "The Answer" back in his college days at Georgetown, because the game was searching for the next big thing; its next star after legends like Bird, Magic and Jordan (at least for a moment) stepped away. Iverson delivered. Rookie of the Year. MVP. He was a fearless, undersized scorer who didn't back down from anyone, not even MJ himself. For us, he was the answer.

Unapologetically himself. True and authentic, and just real. Even with all the criticism about his image and the bias he faced, it was his skill and impact that led the way and cemented his status as a cultural icon.

Fast forward to today, a new "AI" has taken the world by storm, but this time, it comes with algorithms instead of arm sleeves. It wears robots instead of Reeboks. It's Artificial Intelligence. The Answer to eliminating bias in hiring, but does this new AI have the capability to recognize the Iversons of the world, or is it another obstacle in the battle against bias?

Artificial Intelligence isn't the future. It's the right now. What once felt like sci-fi or something imaged out of 'The Jetsons', smart machines, video calls, systems that predict your next move is no longer a cartoon concept. It's our everyday reality. AI is already curating our playlists, filling our feeds with pop-up ads, powering the chatbots that respond before we even finish typing. Whether we realize it or not, AI is everywhere. It's in how we live, how we move, how we connect, and definitely how we work. It's no longer just a tool. It's a cultural and a corporate powerhouse.

Naturally, companies didn't waste any time. Just like we turn to AI to make everyday life easier, from ordering groceries, finding music or asking a digital assistant about the weather. Corporations jumped at the chance to use it to run leaner and faster. Like most tech trends, it didn't take long before AI landed in HR, especially in recruiting. These days, artificial intelligence isn't just on the sidelines, it's in the game. According to Eightfold.ai's 2022 Future of Work survey, 73% of HR leaders said they were already using AI in recruiting, and 92% planned to use even more.

Generative AI now helps teams write job descriptions, auto-generate outreach messages, create pre-screen questions and even rank candidates before a human ever sees their name. Resume screening bots, automated assessments, matching tools, etc. This is the new normal. They cut down on busywork, save time and give teams breathing room when juggling dozens of tasks, but there's a deeper issue we can't ignore.

If we're not careful, we're going to bake the same biases we've always had, into the systems we're relying on to be "fair." That's the catch. Algorithms don't eliminate bias; they reflect the humans who use them. So, while AI might promise to level the playing field, it can just as easily reinforce the same broken patterns, only faster and quieter. That's the part keeping both job seekers and business leaders up at night.

How to Crack the Code to Bias in Hiring

Let's focus on what you can control, but first, let's keep it real. Bias hasn't vanished, if anything, it's gotten bolder. With all the economic shifts and a noticeable rollback in many DEI efforts, the support systems that once helped underrepresented job seekers feel like they're fading fast.

Here's the truth. You may not be able to change how someone sees you. You might not have the power to fix the world around you, but what you do have is the ability to own your approach, tell your story your way and protect your peace while doing it.

That's the key. Focusing on what you can control gives you power. It helps you walk into any room with more clarity, more confidence and more conviction. Not just as your authentic self, but as your best self.

Let's talk about how to do exactly that.

Let Your Online Brand Speak First

People are going to look you up before they meet you. Whether that feels right or not, it's the reality of the modern-day digital world we live in. Before you ever walk into an interview or say a single word, someone's already Googled you or at least pulled up your LinkedIn profile. If we're being honest, you've probably done the same. Just think about it; if you're interested in dating someone, you'll probably try to find their Instagram. At a conference and curious about a speaker? You look them up before choosing their session. That's just how we operate now. We do this every day, so we shouldn't be surprised at all when hiring teams do the same. I'm not saying it's right, it's just reality.

If you've got social media, you've got a digital brand, whether you like it or not. Assumptions are often made before you even walk in the room. Someone already having a bias viewpoint, whether it is intentional or not, will look for signals to confirm their pre-conceived notions. This is where your digital brand comes in. You can either confirm a bias or you can disrupt it. Post content that subtly showcases your knowledge, expertise, passions or what is important to you. It can be a quick video, sharing something you've learned, or a post breaking down an article you read. It doesn't need to be perfect or overly polished. Your digital brand isn't about faking anything.

It's about being intentional and allowing your knowledge, personality and value to shine through. You don't have to overshare; you don't have to be an influencer. You don't need to scream, 'I'm good at what I do.' Let your digital brand do the talking for you. Sometimes, the very person who held a biased opinion of you might scroll through your content, feel a connection and start seeing your value in a whole new light.

Use the Rooms That Were Built for You

One of the best moves you can make for yourself is to get involved with a career-focused organization that's built to support professionals from underrepresented communities. Don't just join. Show up. The real impact doesn't come from adding your name to a membership roster. The real value comes when you engage.

These organizations have local chapters in cities all over the country and were created to give you access, support and a sense of community in spaces where you've often been overlooked. I've seen the value of these organizations both as a member and as a leader. One connection through a professional organization introduced me to a mentor who changed the trajectory of my career. Later, as a President and board member, I helped create those same opportunities for others, making sure doors were opening to opportunities for people who are too often left out of the conversation.

These organizations do more than just host networking events, and mixers; they create platforms. They provide mentorship, offer real connections to job opportunities, and partner with companies who are serious about hiring diverse talent. Here's why that matters. In a world where bias can block access, these rooms are already pre-vetted. The companies that show up at these events are already mission aligned and intentional about trying to reach diverse talent.

So, when you show up in these spaces, you're stepping into rooms where people already value what you bring to the table. You're reducing the gap between opportunity and access and putting yourself in a position to be seen, heard and hired for who you are.

Do a Quick Culture Check

Just like they're going to Google you, you need to Google the company too. Don't take a company's inclusivity at face value just because they posted a few statements or included a few buzzwords here and there on the job description and website. Now don't get me wrong; seeing that kind of language can feel affirming, especially when you're looking for signs that a workplace is inclusive and forward-thinking. Honestly, I do believe there are companies that genuinely care and are putting in the work. I've even helped build some of those efforts myself and I know the efforts are real and not just copied and pasted just to check off a box. There's real strategy, real people and real intention behind it.

Look at where they show up, and how they show up. Are they partnering with organizations that support underrepresented talent? Are they showing up at conferences and events built for people like you, not just to talk, but to hire, mentor and build relationships? Are they putting in time? Are they sponsoring? These are the signals that tell you whether the culture they promote actually holds up in practice.

The vetting goes both ways. That shift In your mindset Is where your power Is. And when you do find the ones who are walking the talk, lean into those companies. Because they're not just talking about equity, they're building spaces where you can feel seen and heard.

Ideas have consequences. And because they do, the ideas shaping your hiring process need inclusion and diverse perspectives at the table, so that more than just one worldview is being shared. Inclusion is about making sure the voices shaping the company reflect the world outside our walls. Whose world you might ask? Everybody's world.

Here's the truth. Too often, many companies love to talk about culture, but they rarely talk about values. And when "culture fit" becomes the standard, it often means "do they act like me, think like me, like what I like?" Your lens is a mirror, often looking for someone who reflects yourself. It should be about "culture add", not "culture fit". Culture add means do they bring us something new that we need. Something that we've been missing.

Inclusion and minimizing bias doesn't start with a software tool. It starts with people. How we listen, how we engage, and how willing we are to make space for someone whose story looks different than ours. If we need a blind resume to give someone a fair shot, that's not innovation. Do we really need a machine to help us treat people fairly? Even then, the machine doesn't even get it right. While technology is helpful for many things, this is not a problem an algorithm can solve. It's something we need to fix within ourselves.

Recruiting is personal. It should be. As a recruiter, you're not just filling jobs. You're shaping culture. You're influencing someone's future, and every time we pass on someone because they don't fit a mold that our pre-conceived notions have formed, we miss out on more than just talent. We miss out on progress.

We should want to learn someone's name. We should want to learn their story. We should be excited to introduce them to our culture and be willing to let their presence evolve it for the better. It matters when we miss a great candidate.

Chapter 10

Reasonable Doubt
The Right to Remain Confident

Reason #10: Lack of Confidence

There's a reason I titled this chapter *Reasonable Doubt*. Not just because it nods to one of the most iconic debut albums in hip-hop history, but because it captures the exact feeling that creeps in when your confidence is under attack. That inner tension. That self-questioning. That battle between what you know you're capable of and what the world is trying to make you believe.

On Jay-Z's *Reasonable Doubt*, the hunger was undeniable. He knew he was great; he just needed the world to catch up, but in between the bars and the bravado were glimpses of something deeper. A man navigating high pressure, high stakes and high expectations. That same pressure shows up in the job search; and just like Jay-Z, you might have the talent, the vision, the work ethic, but you still find yourself having to prove it over and over again.

In the job market, it often feels like you're stuck between *Can't Knock the Hustle* and *Can I Live*; two standout tracks from the Reasonable Doubt album that capture the hunger and heart of the hustle. You're grinding every day, doing all the right things, trying to stay solid while the world throws distractions, doubts and closed doors your way. On one hand, you want to be respected for your effort and consistency. On the other, you just want the space to breathe, to be seen, to exist fully in your purpose without having to explain or justify every move. That's the real hustle. The hustle to stay confident, even when the process seems to wear you down.

Embarking on a job search is a full-time grind. Whether you're fresh out of school, shifting careers, or bouncing back after a layoff, it'll test you. Confidence doesn't always come easy when rejection emails start piling up, interview anxiety creeps in, and you start replaying past failures like highlights on SportsCenter. It wears on even the strongest among us.

I've seen it from both sides. As a recruiter, I've watched qualified people dim their light mid-interview because of doubt. I've had hiring managers root for candidates who just couldn't get out of their own heads. And as a job seeker, I've felt that pressure too. I've hit "submit" on applications and questioned if anyone would even open them. I've avoided my inbox, fearing another automated "thanks, but no thanks" that might knock the wind out of me one more time.

In this game of recruiting, I've put in the work. I've built a name, earned my stripes, and became a trusted voice in the industry. But don't get it twisted. I've also had to lace up and walk that other path too. I've been the job seeker, facing the unknown, navigating setbacks I didn't see coming. Life has its seasons, and no matter how many accolades you've stacked, the winds can shift in an instant.

I know that quiet hesitation when your email notification pings and your stomach sinks because you already know it's another "we regret to inform you." I've been there, avoiding my inbox like its bad news waiting to happen.

Here's what I've learned through all of it. Confidence isn't about pretending everything's perfect. It's knowing that your journey, your hustle and your growth have value, even if it takes the world a little time to catch on.

So, this chapter? It's for anybody who's ever questioned if they're good enough. It's for the overqualified candidates getting overlooked. The laid-off professionals rebuilding from scratch. The high achievers who still have silent doubts. This is about reclaiming your confidence, protecting your peace, and walking into every opportunity like you belong there.

The Constant Urge to Downplay

Don't make yourself small when you should be standing tall. This has nothing to do with your physical height. This is about presence. It's about confidence. It's about fully showing up when the spotlight is finally on you.

In my career, I've seen this play out more times than I can count. Talented people: smart, capable and experienced shrinking themselves down in interviews, almost apologizing for their greatness. Some sat across from hiring panels with a resume full of receipts, yet their spirit didn't walk into the room with them. It's like their confidence got stuck outside the door.

I've come to conclude that one of the hardest human struggles is belief. Belief in a higher power. Belief in others, and most of all, belief in yourself, especially when the world around you keeps giving you reasons to second-guess that belief.

When the "We regret to inform you…" emails keep stacking up.

When you've had interviews where you walked away thinking you nailed it, only to never hear back.

When your past workplace experiences left bruises that never fully healed.

When society constantly teaches you to be "humble," to not make others uncomfortable with your excellence.

All of that can show up in an interview without you even realizing it.

The truth is that hiring managers, recruiters and even peers can feel that energy. When you downplay your wins, brush off your accomplishments or speak like you don't belong there, it shifts the whole dynamic, and not in your favor.

You weren't invited to that interview just to sit quietly and hope they see your potential. You were invited to speak on your value. When you speak, your presence should match your resume. Your wins are not a coincidence. You are not where you are by accident.

I've seen the most impressive candidates miss out, not because they lacked experience, but because they lacked belief. Because somewhere along the way, someone convinced them that being proud meant being arrogant. Or that confidence was a risk. Or that speaking boldly about their success would make them "too much."

You don't need to pretend like you didn't lead that project when you did.

You don't need to say, "I just helped," when you actually led the whole thing.

You don't need to say, "We accomplished..." when you were the one who got it across the finish line.

There's a difference between arrogance and assurance. You don't have to choose between humility and confidence; you can walk in both.

In this next section, I'm going to break down some of the ways this urge to downplay shows up in interviews. Things I've witnessed time and time again that signal a lack of confidence or missed opportunity.

Self-Deprecating to Come Off as Humble:

Downplaying dressed up as humility. It shows up in the form of phrases like *"I guess I just got lucky"* or *"I'm honestly surprised I even pulled that off."* You've seen it. You may have even said it, but the truth is every time you treat your own win like it was just a fluke, you chip away at your credibility. What might feel like being modest or humble to you, might actually be sending a signal to the interviewer that you don't believe in your own greatness. If you don't believe in it, why should they? If you think your success is a fluke, so will others.

Saying "We" Too Much Instead of "I":

Yes, teamwork makes the dream work but let's be clear, your team isn't sitting in that interview seat with you. You are. While it's great to uplift the group and share the shine, this moment is about you. What did you do? What role did you play? Don't downplay your part in a project by constantly defaulting to "we" when it was your late nights, your strategy, your execution that helped bring it across the finish line.

Sometimes, especially for those of us who've been taught not to brag or outshine others, there's a hesitation to speak up for ourselves. Humility doesn't mean invisibility. If you don't clearly claim your contribution, the interviewer may assume you didn't have one. That's how people get passed over.

Apologizing for a Job Well Done:

You'd be surprised how many people downplay their shine by ending their answers with, *"I don't want to sound arrogant"* or *"I'm sorry if that came off like I'm bragging."* Why apologize for what you've earned? You put in the work. You delivered. You showed up and showed out. That's not arrogance, that's receipts. If you were asked to talk about your accomplishments, then do it without shrinking. Interviewers are literally asking for the recap of your highlight reel, not your disclaimer. Confidence isn't the same thing as cockiness, and humility doesn't mean you should hide.

Please don't shrink yourself or fumble a good opportunity just to be perceived a certain way. I get it, nobody wants to come off as cocky in an interview, and believe me, I've seen my fair share of arrogant candidates, but let's be real, confidence and arrogance are not the same thing. Confidence is not arrogance, it's presence.

Yes, it's a fine line to walk, no doubt, but some of the most powerful things in life live in that balance. Confidence, in its truest form, is the blending gratefulness with fruitfulness. What do I mean by that? I've learned through my own journey that being grateful doesn't mean you downplay your gifts. It means you honor them. You can give thanks for your blessings, and at the same time, speak boldly about the impact those blessings have had on your work, career, and community.

That, to me, is what real confidence looks like. It's knowing you've done the work and standing tall in that truth. So as we move forward, let's go a little deeper into what confidence really means, how it shows up, and why it matters more now than ever.

How To Crack the Code to Lacking Confidence

What is confidence, exactly? Sure, there are plenty of mainstream definitions floating around. Images of loud bravado, puffed-out chests and over the top energy that demands the room's attention, but let's be real. That's not confidence. That's performance. Performance without purpose fades fast.

I've got my own definition. Confidence, to me, isn't about intimidation or flexing for validation. It's about depth. It's about alignment. And most of all, it's about truth.

- **Clarity** means you know exactly who you are.
- **Ownership** means you fully embrace and stand on what you're good at.
- **Awareness** means you understand the positive impact of your gifts on yourself and the people around you.

When those three meet, that's the intersection where real confidence lives. It's not performative, it's rooted. It's not loud, it's certain.

Let's break it down. Confidence is a mix of Clarity + Ownership + Awareness.

Clarity starts with knowing who you are at the core. Your values. Your principles. Your beliefs. Even your boundaries. You can't walk in confidence if you don't have clarity. In both career and life, self-awareness is the foundation of self-assurance.

Then there's *Ownership*. This is where a lot of people hesitate. It's one thing to know what you're good at, but an entirely different thing to own it. Are you constantly brushing off compliments, shrinking back or second-guessing your wins? True ownership is standing ten toes down in your abilities without needing to apologize or downplay a thing.

And finally, Awareness. This is the part that often gets overlooked. It's knowing that your skills, your energy, your way of showing up matters. It helps people. It moves the needle. It brings value. When you're aware of the influence you carry, you begin to move different. You speak with intention. You show up with presence.

Put it all together, and that's what real, authentic confidence looks like. It's not hype. It's harmony. It's not arrogance. It's alignment, and the beauty of it? Anyone can build it. Because it doesn't come from outside validation, it comes from within.

There's always that moment in every job search, sometimes more than one where someone in your network drops that all-too-familiar LinkedIn update: "I'm happy to announce…" Cue the digital confetti, a shiny new title, a fresh company logo and a flood of likes and clapping hands in the comments.

Now listen, we love to see it. Truly. It's inspiring to witness people step into new chapters, to see doors open for folks we know and admire. The reality is that it's also completely human to feel that quiet sting in the background, the little voice that whispers, *"What about me?"* or *"When's it going to be my turn?"*

You're showing up. You're doing the right things. You're applying. You're networking. You're interviewing. Still, the self-doubt creeps in. You start wondering: *Am I missing something? Maybe I'm not who I thought I was. Maybe I don't fit the mold anymore.*

I've had people open up and tell me they felt so defeated that they started to believe their career was over. And I'll keep it real with you, I've been there too. They say comparison is the thief of joy. Let's go a step deeper. It's also the silent killer of confidence. What we don't talk about enough are those quiet in-between moments. That emotional stretch between your last opportunity and your next one. It's not fun. It's not flashy. It's far from easy, but it's real.

The good news? Confidence can be rebuilt. Protected. Reinforced. Even when everything around you feels uncertain. Especially then. Confidence isn't just something you have when the sun is shining. It's something you grow in the rain. It's a muscle. Like any muscle, it needs work, care and recovery.

Now let's talk about how to do just that. How to protect your peace, feed your confidence and rewrite the narrative, even in the storm.

Stay in Motion

Just because the job search isn't moving how you want it to, doesn't mean you have to stand still. This is the time to shine in other areas of your life that still deserve your light. Join a volunteer group. Sit on a board or committee for a cause that speaks to your soul. Or finally start that blog, podcast, or content series that's been living in your notes app for way too long. Do something that showcases your passion, purpose, and skills on your terms.

No, it might not land you a job tomorrow, but it will give you momentum; and momentum builds belief. With every small win, you start to trust yourself again. You start to remember what you're made of. That's what confidence is really built on, not just wins in your career, but motion in your life. Your worth was never meant to be tied up in just your job title. It's something I even mentioned back in 2023 when I was featured in a *CNBC article* about this topic; and it bears repeating here. Keep moving. Keep giving. Keep building, because the value you bring to the world exists far beyond your 9 to 5.

Less Hustle, More Focus

Spending all day, every day applying for jobs will wear you down fast. It drains you mentally and emotionally, and chips away at your confidence. Instead of applying every hour on the hour, set aside just part of your day to intentionally focus on your job search. For example, block off your mornings and set a realistic, high-quality goal for how many applications and follow up emails you want to send out. The aim is to prioritize quality over quantity. Once you hit your target, shut it down for the day. Go do something else not related to your search. Hit the gym. Take a walk. Grab a matcha latte at your favorite coffee spot. Go to a game night and play Spades; or all the above. Just do something else!

While this piece of advice may go against the usual go-hard advice in our culture, I would argue my proposed approach actually builds confidence. Why? Because it will remind you that even in the uncertainty, you still have control over your time, your energy, and how you take care of yourself.

Remember Who You Are

The silence during the job search can be deafening, but the right voices in your corner can drown it out. That's why your circle matters. The MVPs we talked about earlier? This is where they show up. These are the people who know your story, your heart and your journey. They remind you of your worth when you're too weighed down to remember it yourself. They don't play about you.

Yes, the work is yours to do, but let's not act like anyone gets through this alone. We all crave that confidence boost that comes with the job offer email or that final round congratulations call. But until then? That boost can come from the people who see the best in you, even when you're feeling your lowest. Maybe it's your mentor who reminds you of how you held your own during that chaotic product launch as a junior associate, keeping the whole squad aligned. Maybe it's your coach who's watched you prep like a pro and knows, deep down, that when your time comes, you won't fold. Maybe it's your spouse, your mother, or your best friend sending you daily affirmations, or your partner who prays over you before you close your eyes at night.

Whoever they are, identify them, cherish them and lean on them. Because real confidence isn't built in isolation, it's strengthened in community. Keep your people close. They're part of the reason you'll make it to the other side.

At the end of the day, some interview questions hit harder than others. Over the years as a recruiter, I've seen certain questions consistently throw candidates off their game. Even though I'm usually the one on the other side of the table or screen, I still understand the pressure. You want to make a strong impression, you want to be seen and let's be honest, you want to land the job.

Two questions in particular tend to rattle even the most qualified professionals: the ones about unexplained gaps in employment, and what some perceive as job hopping. It's that moment when someone glances at your resume and raises an eyebrow over three roles in four years, even when every move made sense and was rooted in strategy, survival or growth.

The nerves? Understandable. The fear of judgment? Very real, but these questions don't have to shake your confidence. With a little preparation, a clear mindset and the right framing, you can answer them with poise and power. Let's walk through how to do just that.

Keep It Real, But Keep It Moving

When asked about a gap or multiple moves on your resume, give a concise, honest explanation. There's no need for a deep documentary-style breakdown. You don't have to give them the whole play-by-play like a sports analyst dissecting every quarter of the game. Say what needs to be said, take ownership and pivot. The goal is to acknowledge the moment without letting it take over the whole interview. Show that you've reflected, grown, and are ready for what's next. Keep it clear, confident, and forward-facing because the story isn't about the gap, it's about the growth.

Check the Tone, Not the Truth

Keep it professional by checking your tone. That layoff you went through might've been rough, or maybe you're still low-key irritated about how often people question the moves you've made, but don't let that frustration spill into your answers. Even if the experience was unfair, and even if you've got every right to be frustrated, this moment isn't the time to air it out. Stay calm, poised and in control. How you talk about your journey matters. If you're at peace with the path you've taken, even with the bumps and pivots, it sends a clear message, confidence. Not in perfection, but in progress.

Shift the Focus to What You Bring to the Table

When that moment comes in the interview and they ask about the gap or why you moved around a bit, don't get stuck replaying the past like it's a documentary. Instead, flip the script. Prioritize showing your value over defending your journey.

The goal isn't to justify every decision or explain every twist and turn. It's to make it clear that you've learned, grown, and you're ready to contribute right now. Speak on the skills you gained, the lessons you took with you, and how all of that lines up with what they actually need in this role.

When you do that, you take control of the conversation. You stop playing defense and start showing up with ownership and purpose. And that's the energy that makes hiring managers lean in.

One day, I chimed in on a post from a well-known tech influencer who was sharing tips on how to handle the "job-hopping" question in interviews. As someone who's been a trusted voice in his network and even a guest on his podcast—yes, the same podcast I mentioned back in one of the earlier chapters, I felt comfortable offering my own perspective in the comments. What I didn't expect was how well it would resonate. Not only did he respond positively, but the comment took off, gaining over a thousand likes and dozens of positive responses from his followers. Below is what I posted, and an example of how to frame an answer to that specific question about job-hopping.

"In that timeframe, I was presented with new challenges & professional growth opportunities. After much consideration, I embraced these experiences which equipped me with valuable skills and knowledge that attracted you to my resume. I believe these gained skills will bring an immediate positive impact on both this role and your company."

Remember that confidence is not about having the perfect story, because the truth is, no one does. Even the people you admire, the ones who seem to have it all figured out, have had their own twists, turns and unexpected pauses along the way. What sets them apart is that they kept going. They faced their doubts head-on and leaned on the right people to help them confront whatever transitions were needed to endure.

Confidence is about unapologetically owning your journey and every part of it. So, stand tall, stay grounded, honor the people who've walked with you and most important of all, know thyself.

Just like the classic Jay-Z album *Reasonable Doubt*, which this chapter is named after, you don't need everyone to see the vision at first. That album didn't go platinum right away, but those who really knew, recognized its genius from the jump. Songs like *"Can't Knock the Hustle"* and *"Can I Live"* weren't just records, they were anthems for anyone moving through the world with purpose and pressure on their back. Just like Jay-Z, you don't have to explain your grind to everybody, and you don't need to shrink your shine for people who can't handle your light.

You're not just chasing a job. You're chasing alignment. Protect your peace. Prioritize your growth. Cement your legacy.

You've earned the right to remain confident.

Conclusion

This Was Never Just About a Job

By now, you've read the stories, soaked in the strategies, and started to see both the job search and yourself through a new lens. But let's be clear… this book was never just about landing a role.

It's about showing up for yourself in ways you didn't always have the language, the tools, or the confidence to do before.

It's about remembering that your resume is more than a document, it's your *hype reel*.

That networking isn't just about asking, it's about *offering value*.

That storytelling isn't just a soft skill. It's your *superpower* in interviews.

And that confidence? It's not arrogance. It's *presence*. It's knowing who you are, owning what you bring, and being fully aware of the impact you can make.

I wrote this book because I've lived every angle of this game; job seeker, recruiter, hiring manager and talent strategist. I've sat in those chairs on multiple sides of the table. I've witnessed how brilliant people fumble opportunities in interviews not because they weren't good enough, but because they didn't believe they were. I've seen how overlooked resumes get passed over, not because they lacked talent, but because they didn't tell the story right.

And I've also seen how people rise when they're given the truth, the insight and the hope to believe in themselves again.

To my fellow recruiters and hiring professionals reading this, I hope this book gave you something too. A reminder of the human behind the application. A challenge to reflect on how we evaluate talent and how we show up for people in the process. Let this be a push to lead with more empathy, more clarity and more commitment to creating space where excellence in all its forms can thrive. We have the power to influence outcomes that change lives. Let's never take that lightly.

To the job seeker, the career pivoter, the one who's been laid off or the one simply looking for a chance, this was for you. For the ones who were told to stay humble and ended up downplaying themselves in every interview; for the ones who second-guessed their story because it didn't look traditional; for the ones who are tired, but still pushing, this is also for you.

Let this be your reminder:

You've got receipts.
You've got range.
You've got value.
You've got the right to remain confident.

Take everything you've learned in these pages, everything you've experienced in your journey and go *crack the code* on what's next.

— *Bobby McNeil Jr.*

Notes

Behavioral Based Interviewing – SHRM (Society of Human Resource Management)
https://www.shrm.org/topics-tools/news/career-advice-qa/how-to-answer-behavioral-interview-questions-get-job-offers#:~:text=Behavioral%20interview%20strategy%20bases%20questions,events%20in%20their%20work%20history.

The Future of Work: Intelligent by Design Eightfold AI's 2022 Talent Survey
https://eightfold.ai/wp-content/uploads/2022_Talent_Survey.pdf

DDI STAR Method
https://www.ddiworld.com/solutions/behavioral-interviewing/star-method#:~:text=DDI%20invented%20the%20STAR%20method,interview%20or%20when%20providing%20feedback.

The Deming Institute - PDCA
https://deming.org/explore/pdsa/

ASQ - Fishbone
https://asq.org/quality-resources/fishbone

Ways AI is Changing HR Departments
https://www.businessnewsdaily.com/how-ai-is-changing-hr

Closing the Digital Skills Divide – Federal Reserve Bank of Atlanta, April 6th, 2023
https://nationalskillscoalition.org/wp-content/uploads/2023/02/NSC-DigitalDivide_report_Feb2023.pdf

ACLU – How Artificial Intelligence Might Prevent You From Getting Hired
https://www.aclu.org/news/racial-justice/how-artificial-intelligence-might-prevent-you-from-getting-hired

12 types of hiring bias and how to avoid them – Homerun
https://www.homerun.co/articles/4-types-of-hiring-bias-and-how-to-avoid-them

Acknowledgments

First and foremost, I want to express deep gratitude to every single person who poured into me, encouraged me, challenged me and helped shape the journey that led to this book. *Cracking the Code* isn't just the result of late nights and long weekends, it's the product of years of lived experience, sacrifice, community, wisdom and countless conversations that pushed me to think deeper and write with purpose.

There have been so many people along the way, some who were a part of my career journey from day one and others who joined me specifically for this book. Whether you were there helping me shape ideas, reminding me to keep going or just being along for the ride, your presence mattered. You helped make this real.

To every candidate who trusted me, every hiring manager who collaborated with me, every mentor who believed in me and every friend or peer who said, "You should put this in a book", thank you. Your stories, your belief and your support are embedded into every page.

To my family — ***Mom, Dad, Tawane, and Jamaal*** — thank you for being my rock and my roots. Your love, patience, belief, and countless prayers carried me through every season of life and every sentence of this book. I couldn't have done this without you.

To **Rich Gilliam** — your encouragement, your loyalty, and your friendship. You always showed up. The calls, the check-ins, the real talks, and that key introduction to our publisher. I'll never forget it. A shared mission brought us together, but this journey of authorship made us brothers. Thank you!

To ***every podcast host, panel organizer, and conference curator*** — *too many to name, but you know who you are.* Thank you for handing me the mic and creating space for these conversations to live. Every opportunity to speak helped plant the seeds that grew into this book.

To **Cyrus Harbin** — your platform took me to a level I never saw coming. Thank you for seeing me, for believing in me, and for letting me speak to your community. That episode changed everything. Since that day on the pod, it's been up ever since. I appreciate you, fam.

To **Brentley Wright** – you're an incredible man of faith. Your walk with God and the way you lead by example have been truly inspiring to fellow believers like me. Thank you for the affirmations, the prayers, and the words of encouragement you've spoken over me. Your passion for God and your heart for making people feel included have deeply influenced me. I see you, and I thank you bro.

To **_Grace Morris_** — thank you for everything. Some people cross paths with you for a moment but leave a lasting impact. You were that for me.

To **_every reader,_** whether you're a job seeker trying to bounce back, a recruiter sharpening your craft, a hiring leader looking for perspective, or someone just trying to figure out the next step. Thank you for picking up this book. My prayer is that these pages make you feel seen, empowered, and more confident about your journey.

About the Author

Bobby McNeil Jr. is a nationally recognized, award-winning Talent Acquisition Leader, author, and community leader who has spent over a decade using his platform to elevate others. With a career rooted in corporate excellence and cultural empowerment, Bobby has become one of the most trusted voices in the talent space, respected for how he builds, connects, and leads.

He's not just walked the path; he's built bridges along the way. He's helped people get hired across functions, industries, and experience levels. His ability to connect real people to real opportunities has earned him national respect.

As former President of the award-winning Blacks In Technology's Raleigh-Durham Chapter, 2023 IMPACT Award Winner and 2024 Chapter of the Year under his leadership, Bobby spearheaded impactful programming that empowered Black technologists across the region. Today, he serves as a Vice President for the National Black MBA Association's Raleigh-Durham Triad Chapter, where he continues to assist in building new pipelines for leadership, access and economic mobility.

A former high school basketball standout in Fuquay-Varina, North Carolina and NCAA Division II National Champion with Barton College, Bobby brings the same grit, teamwork and resilience to every professional endeavor. He graduated with honors (Cum Laude) in Business Administration and still carries that student-athlete mindset: stay ready, stay humble and outwork the doubt.

Bobby's influence goes far beyond resumes and interviews. He's spoken at major conferences, been featured on national podcasts and was named one of LinkedIn's Power 50 Top Black Creators. In 2023, he was also featured in CNBC News for his insights on career development and job search confidence. He currently serves on the Board of Advisors for the North Carolina Technology Association, where he helps bridge corporate strategy with community impact.

What makes Bobby different isn't just what he does, it's how he does it. He leads with clarity, compassion and conviction. His leadership is authentic, culturally grounded and always people-first. He's that rare mix of recruiting leader, mentor, strategist and storyteller.

Whether you're reading his words or listening to him speak, Bobby shows up with heart and purpose. He doesn't just share insights, he shares truth. He doesn't just talk about access, he makes it happen. For Bobby, success isn't just about personal wins, it's about creating pathways for others to walk through confidently.